Praise for *Illuminating Sermons*

I headed to the church parking lot after having preached during our 11:00 a.m. worship service, and an usher jokingly asked, "Did you get your book back?" She saw the confused look on my face. She laughed and said, "The book you talked about in the sermon. Did you get it back?" I laughed, too. Her husband also laughed out loud and said, "Pastor, that was a great story. People will remember that one for a long time."

Those two beloved church members made the point of *Illuminating Sermons*: Stories stick. Carlos E. Wilton takes readers on a masterful but very practical journey in helping preachers become curators who create, for their sermonic disposal, a cadre of tools for illumination, not just illustration. As someone who regularly preaches, I found Wilton's guidance, in a category-by-category form, essential for moving from high-level abstraction to concrete illumination. This book is a great tool for anyone serious about preaching and using it to transform people's lives. I highly recommend *Illuminating Sermons*.

—**Rev. Dr. Jonathan C. Augustine**, senior pastor of St. Joseph AME Church, Durham, North Carolina, and author of *When Prophets Preach: Leadership and the Politics of the Pulpit*; and inductee of the Morehouse College Martin Luther King Jr. Board of Preachers

The ability to make a sermon more relatable with illustrations is essential. But often illustrations are hard to come by. *Illuminating Sermons* gives the preacher necessary tools that make illustration-finding easier. It is a key tool in the preacher's arsenal.

—**Rev. Dr. Marcus Jerkins**, senior pastor of New Pilgrim Baptist Church, Birmingham, Alabama, and author of *Black Lives Matter to Jesus: The Salvation of Black Life and All Life in Luke and Acts*

This practical and well-written book will be an excellent resource for preachers at all stages of their ministry. It reflects Carlos E. Wilton's vast pastoral experience and excellent judgment. Wilton has gathered here a resource that teaches how to locate, choose, present, and archive appropriate sermon illustrations.

—**Rev. Dr. Doreen M. McFarlane**, ELCIC pastor; coauthor of *The People Are Holy: The History and Theology of Free Church Worship*, and author of the forthcoming *God in Translation: The Theological Gifts of Exploring Biblical Languages*

Illuminating Sermons

Illuminating Sermons

Curating Illustrations That Inspire

Carlos E. Wilton

FORTRESS PRESS
MINNEAPOLIS

ILLUMINATING SERMONS
Curating Illustrations That Inspire

30 29 28 27 26 25 1 2 3 4 5 6 7 8 9

Library of Congress Control Number: 2025934217 (print)

Cover design: Angela Griner
Cover image: Design for Light in Chapter Room, Carnegie Hall, New York, NY, Alice Cordelia Morse, via Smithsonian Design Museum, Gift of Alice C. Morse ca. 1890

Print ISBN: 979-8-8898-3495-3
eBook ISBN: 979-8-8898-3496-0

For Claire

Contents

Preface ix

Introduction: The Illuminator's Art 1
- Curating Wonder 3
- Grow Your Own 7
- Illumination, Not Illustration 9
- Borrowed Light 12
- Thus Says the Lord 15
- The Homiletical Helix 20

1. The Collector: Chasing the Shimmer 25
   - The Ladder of Abstraction 30
   - Bessie the Cow 31
   - Concretion Is Incarnational 34
   - Places That Shimmer 41

2. The Taxonomist: Tagging Your Finds 45
   - The Wand Finds the Wizard 46
   - Lessons from the *Beagle* 48
   - Labyrinths and Cold Frames 50
   - From Bottom Drawer to Database 52

3. The Librarian: Tapping Your Collection 59
   - Old Men Will Dream Dreams 62
   - Reigniting the Shimmer 66

4. The Collaborator: Borrowing with Integrity 69
   - You Can't Fake Authenticity 71
   - Invasion of the Avatars 76

5. The Designer: Imagining the Sequence 81
One More Stone in the Wall 82
Envisioning Through a Storyboard 84

6. The Exhibitor: Inviting Wonder 111
To Build a Fire 114
The Knight's Move 123
Trust Your Peripheral Vision 131
Playing Language Games 136
The Preacher as Docent 138
Preach Like a Playwright 142
An Illumination Toolbox 147

7. The Archivist: Preparing for Another Sermon 165

Postscript 171

Preface

So, where do you find good sermon illustrations?

If you're a preacher, you've been there. You've posed that question to the universe, late on a Saturday evening. It's not that your seminary professors didn't teach you well. Your exegesis is sound. Your message is logical, clearly stated and relevant to human need. But something's missing: a spark to ignite imagination, to *illuminate* the sermon.

You've combed through published anthologies of sermon illustrations, either in book form or on the internet. There you've unearthed the occasional treasure, but to reach it you've had to shovel away a great deal of brown earth—stale or stilted material you could never use. Illustrations anthologies are hit or miss. That's because they're the creative work of others. No matter how good the material, it's hard to make others' work your own.

You know and appreciate the power of a good story, the shape-shifting magic of metaphor. But you also know how hard it is to generate such material on demand. Homiletical gems surface, unsought, in random moments. Suddenly you mutter under your breath, "That'll preach!" But the quicksilver shimmer doesn't stick around for long.

But what if you could find a way to freeze it in time—your own aha moment, not someone else's—and recall it later, just when you need it? Wouldn't that be fine? Week after week, you'd come up with a collection of metaphors, stories, quotations, and poems that cry out "That'll preach!"—not "This'll do."

That's why I've written this book.

Colleagues who know my work describe me as a curator of sermon illustrations. For over fifteen years, I've written most of the illustrations that appear in each issue of *Homiletics Online* (formerly *Homiletics* magazine). I don't pull those illustrations out of thin air. A great many of them come from a database I've kept throughout my preaching ministry that allows me to file promising material under numerous topic words. I could easily dredge my illustrations database to assemble a topically organized greatest hits collection. But that would be no different than the many illustrations anthologies on the market. I don't think the world needs another one of those books.

What I'm offering instead is a process for capturing your own aha moments as they providentially occur, then preserving them for future use precisely when you need them. If you do this well, a great many of your ideas will seem just as fresh as on the day they first ignited your imagination. You'll also find that once you tap your database before your sermon is fully formed, some of these items actually give shape to the sermon rather than simply embellishing it.

For years, I've been thinking deeply about what sermon illustrations are, how they function, and how to curate them so the shimmer of discovery retains its freshness. This book is the product of that reflection. Perhaps the best way to state my purpose is to fracture an all-too-familiar proverb: Give preachers an illustration, and they'll preach for a day; teach them to curate illustrations, and they'll preach for a lifetime.

Introduction

The Illuminator's Art

The Latin root of curation, *cura*, literally means "to take care of." For many years, the best-known use of the word has been the profession of museum curator: a manager responsible for preserving, cataloging, and selectively displaying the museum's holdings. In conceiving and designing special exhibitions, curators are uniquely skilled in bringing out the perfect items from the museum's warehouse to speak to the zeitgeist of the moment.

Effective curation is a remarkable achievement. Museums are charged with maintaining and caring for a multitude of old things. To catalog and then pull out just the right assortment of special-exhibition items to convey an impression of continual freshness—thereby ensuring a steady supply of visitors streaming through the museum's doors—requires, to quote actor Liam Neeson's character in *Taken*, "a very particular set of skills."[1]

It so happens there's a related ecclesiastical term. A curate is a priest in the Episcopal Church—typically younger and inexperienced—who's charged with leading worship in a smaller, subsidiary congregation or who serves a larger church as assistant

1 *Taken*, directed by Pierre Morel (2008, EuropaCorp S.A.).

to the rector. It's a person to whom the rector can delegate certain caretaking tasks.

Cura is also the source of another English term that's foundational to sermon illumination. That word is *curiosity.* We're curious about things we care about. Our search for sermon illumination material is a practical application of curiosity.

The noun *curiosity* has two meanings. The most common is our human capacity for wonder that causes us to value new experiences. The second denotes a tangible object that calls forth feelings of curiosity. Early naturalists of the Enlightenment era—as well as the noble patrons who bankrolled their work—maintained cabinets of curiosities. These were small rooms in which they would display novel items gathered on journeys of discovery: semiprecious stones, narwhal tusks, rare butterflies, votive objects belonging to other cultures—anything that sparked fascination and wonder. Cabinets of curiosities were the ancestors of today's natural history museums. Today, they're a model for our collections of sermon illumination material.

One of the most reliable ways to connect with a congregation is to share something that sparks their natural curiosity. Explaining or drawing attention to something from the natural world, history, science, or anything else from the world of human knowledge is a surefire way of enticing curious listeners into deeper curiosity about some aspect of the biblical text. A sermon illumination may appear tangential at first, but once you align a story or example so it runs parallel to some biblical truth, a spark emerges that leaps the synapse, igniting curiosity about what the Bible says.

Curiosity is not where you want your listeners to end up, but it's a crucial step along the way—a gracious invitation. Curiosity functions as the pilot light for imagination. It's but a short step from curiosity to imaginative vision that brings God's word to life.

Of course, curation is by no means unique to preaching. In the early 2020s, the word *curator* was suddenly everywhere. In the years immediately preceding, as the internet became ubiquitous and scrolling through a social media feed felt like drinking from the proverbial fire hose, users with a knack for curating the best content and copying it to their own feed became highly prized. Some have described the skill—borrowing an analogy from audio electronics—as the art of finding signal in the noise.

Jumping on the curation bandwagon, restaurants began advertising curated menus. High-end clothing boutiques touted curated dresses on their racks. Travel agents sold curated tours. A personal organization guru published a book called *The Curated Closet*.

At the risk of sounding merely trendy, I'd like to suggest that curator is an apt descriptor of an essential preaching task: that of gathering, organizing, and maintaining a personal collection of material for illuminating sermons. That collection functions like a museum warehouse. Few patrons have any conception of how many items their favorite museum typically holds, beyond its permanent galleries. The Smithsonian Institution, the world's largest museum, holds more than 150 million objects with only a tiny fraction of them on public display. Likewise, few sermon listeners have any conception of how large a collection of material it takes for their preacher to produce effective sermons week after week.

CURATING WONDER

What you curate, as a preacher, is wonder.

For example, the Scriptures offer a story about a man whose attention was turned aside by wonder. His life was forever changed. The man is Moses. The scene of his epiphany is a threadbare patch of pastureland whose location is lost to history. Moses is doing absolutely nothing out of the ordinary, although his life has been anything but ordinary. Recall his infant voyage in the pitch-caulked basket upon the Nile, his adoption into the royal family, his rediscovery of his Hebrew roots, and his hotheaded murder of an overseer in a misguided search for justice. Moses's most recent cliffhanger is his desperate flight beyond the reach of the pharaoh's rage.

Moses falls in with a band of Midianites. He proves his skill as a shepherd and eventually marries the boss's daughter. Life is good. Not as tumultuous as it once was, in the shadow of the pyramids, but good enough. Until the day he sees a bush ablaze but not consumed:

> Then Moses said, "I must turn aside and look at this great sight and see why the bush is not burned up." When the Lord saw that he had turned aside to see, God called to him out of the bush, "Moses, Moses!" And he said, "Here I am." (Exod 3:3–4)

Notice the sequential steps that take place. First, Moses sees. Second, he makes a conscious decision to turn aside and look more closely. Third (and the Scripture's quite clear on this point), it's only after Moses has consciously turned aside that the Lord addresses him by name.

The Lord could have cut to the chase and simply called out, "Hey Moses, get a load of this bush!" But that's not how God does it. Vision first, then voice. Moses must glimpse the light and turn aside to see it before he can walk the walk, let alone talk the talk.

The Irish have a phrase called *second sight*. To the popular imagination, it means clairvoyance: foretelling the future through a form of extrasensory perception. But what if it simply means lingering for a second look, as Moses does? What if it means looking through the ordinary to see glimmers of the divine?

The bush is not merely ablaze, torched by a bolt of lightning or a poorly extinguished campfire. Desert brushfires are common enough. But this is different. The bush is illuminated. Its unearthly glow emanates from within.

It's a wonder. Having seen it, Moses knows what he has to do. He must share the wonder with others.

Your task as preacher—what your people, to put it bluntly, are paying you to do—is to venture onto the same barren hills as everyone else, chasing after the same ornery livestock, but with an eye out for the unexpected and unaccountable wonder. Your special training equips you not only to trust your peripheral vision but also to pause and ponder the curiosities it reveals. After regarding a numinous wonder for a time, your job is to say to the others, "Come and see!"

New York Times columnist David Brooks pays tribute to the transformative power of his own experiences of spiritual wonder:

> When faith finally tiptoed into my life it didn't come through information or persuasion but, at least at first, through numinous experiences. These are the scattered moments of awe and wonder that wash over most of us unexpectedly from time to time. Looking back over the decades, I remember rare transcendent moments at the foot of a mountain in New England at dawn, at Chartres Cathedral in France, looking at images of the distant universe or of a baby in the womb. In those moments, you have a sense that you are in the presence of something overwhelming, mysterious. Time is suspended or at least blurs. One is enveloped by an enormous bliss.[2]

Numinous experiences of the sort Brooks describes are notoriously difficult to conjure. Most of us would say they just happen unexpectedly. Every once in a while, a sermon of yours may kindle an experience of wild wonder in the imagination of some of your listeners—although you can never count on that happening or even predict which particular words could spark such delight. It's just something that sparkles in the fertile space between your mouth and the congregation's ears, a sacred collaboration between preacher and listener with neither party fully in control.

One thing you can control, however, is the material traditionally known as illustrations. At best, these are small wonders capable of inspiring joy, curiosity, or appreciation of beauty. They appear in the transitions within your sermons—the sometimes

2 David Brooks, "The Shock of Faith: It's Nothing Like I Thought It Would Be," *New York Times*, December 19, 2024, https://www.nytimes.com/2024/12/19/opinion/faith-god-christianity.html.

unexpected changes in direction that signal a come-and-see moment. Small wonders they may be, but they're wonders all the same. But here's something wondrous about wonder: It's scalable. Wonders come in many different sizes, from small to XXXL, but they're made of the same God-given quicksilver stuff. The act of repeatedly turning aside to see them builds spiritual muscle memory in your listeners, alerting them to their own personal epiphanies, large and small.

The language you choose is important. You don't have to put in much time in a seminary classroom before you start picking up the professional lingo. Equipped with such twenty-dollar words, it's not terribly difficult to engage in theological speech—trafficking in divinity, as your diploma smugly promises. Most congregations will tolerate such pedantry from the pulpit. They may even expect it. But their desire, in their heart of hearts, is for something deeper.

What they yearn for is to glimpse the burning bush itself. And they're hoping you'll be the one to guide them to it. In an oft-quoted remark (whose precise provenance I've never been able to nail down) Rabbi Abraham Joshua Heschel is said to have observed:

> Our goal should be to live life in radical amazement, [to] get up in the morning and look at the world in a way that takes nothing for granted. Everything is phenomenal; everything is incredible; never treat life casually. To be spiritual is to be amazed.

To curate sermon material is to traffic in amazement, to live life in a radically open way, noticing and gathering up the manna life bestows. It's the life of a poet, really, as Mary Oliver points out when she famously advises fellow poets to "pay attention, be astonished, tell about it."[3] While not intending to, she's eloquently sounding the rhythms of the preaching life.

---

3 Mary Oliver, "Messenger," in *Thirst: Poems* (Beacon Press, 2006), 1.

GROW YOUR OWN

As a preacher, sacred astonishment is your modus operandi for your curation. But those numinous experiences are never at your beck and call. Amid all this shimmering abundance, you may still find yourself mouthing that perennial, nagging question, Where do I find good illustrations? That's the wrong question to ask.

A better question is, How do I grow them?

There's an organic process to cultivating illustrations over time. It's theological photosynthesis, drawing and converting energy from many aspects of your life.

From this point onward, though, I'll begin talking about the shift away from the language of illustrations. For too long, homiletical orthodoxy has treated sermon illustrations as ornamental, like garnish on a restaurant plate. In fact, illustrations contribute so much more to your listeners' understanding. The best of these metaphors, stories, poems, and quotations don't simply illustrate the theological insights derived from exegesis. They illuminate them.

Illumination evokes the spirit of ancient monks who labored long with paintbrush and pen to make the Scriptures a thing of beauty. Sure, a medieval illuminated manuscript may have a few pictures dropped into it, but the greater part of the illuminator's craft is rendering the words themselves in a special way. Human words and art become as one, lifting up the beauty of God's word.

We'll explore further the metaphor of manuscript illumination momentarily. But first, a bit more about curation as an overarching metaphor for this book, the cup that cradles everything that follows. As I mentioned, museum curators categorize and manage artifacts stacked floor-to-ceiling in hidden warehouses. When it's time to mount a special exhibition, they assemble a select representation of those vast holdings to display for a limited time.

Sermon writing is like that. Think of each weekly message as a new special exhibition. If, over time, you've faithfully tended your illuminations warehouse—assembling a collection of resources that have turned your head and that, soon after discovering them, you've filed away under topic or Scripture citation—you'll never want for good material to cause your listeners to turn their heads and see, to ignite their imagination.

Curation is a complex job. In all but the smallest museums, nobody tries to do it all. True, the museum director sits at a grand desk behind a curator nameplate, but the practical work of curation is divided among a number of specialists. Some of these staffers focus on acquisitions. Others specialize in preservation. Still others manage the vast, out-of-sight warehouse collections. Some design the changing layout of special-exhibition galleries. Others negotiate loans of prized treasures from other museums. Still others manage the patron experience, arranging tours and recruiting docents who guide visitors through the galleries.

Each chapter in this book focuses on a subtask, borrowed from the work of museum curation, that a preacher performs during the larger work of curating sermon illustrations:

- Chapter 1, The Collector: Chasing the Shimmer, focuses on where you can locate sermon material that shimmers, not just for next Sunday's sermon but for sermons yet to come.
- Chapter 2, The Taxonomist: Tagging Your Finds, explores how you warehouse this material, tagging individual items so you can quickly locate them when needed.
- Chapter 3, The Librarian: Tapping Your Collection, deals with how you can search your collection of illustrations for likely prospects for any given sermon and, most importantly, rediscover the shimmer you earlier experienced.
- Chapter 4, The Collaborator: Borrowing with Integrity, notes the ways that great museums borrow from other institutions as they mount their special exhibitions. Following their lead, this chapter covers how you ethically borrow and credit sermon material from others without diluting the authenticity of your own message.

- Chapter 5, The Designer: Imagining the Sequence, covers how you storyboard the best of those selected items in a staging area, narrowing the field to the ones you're most likely to use and then sequencing them in an engaging way.
- Chapter 6, The Exhibitor: Inviting Wonder, explores how using a sermon's scripture text and topic as guides leads listeners through the sermon as though it were an exhibition. This includes focusing on the craft of writing, which is equally necessary whether you bring a full manuscript into the pulpit or preach from notes.
- Chapter 7, The Archivist: Preparing for Another Sermon, emphasizes the importance of returning used illuminations to your archive, retagging as necessary. A few illuminations may be useful in sermons yet to come—perhaps in another congregation. By marking sermon materials as used, you can avoid unconscious repetition.

A final word about the writing style I've employed. Although this book is intended both for academic settings and for individual study, I've avoided the traditional language conventions of the academy. This is intentional. Good homiletical writing avoids jargon and strives to be conversational. I've tried to model that approach, writing this book for speech—keeping sentences short, using the second person extensively, and making liberal use of contractions. I hope you'll receive it as a conversation, one preacher to another.

ILLUMINATION, NOT ILLUSTRATION

We begin in the ninth century CE in a very out-of-the-way place: the scriptorium of a Celtic monastery. What would likely have struck you about the place was its silence. That was odd because—more than most places in the ninth century—this quiet chamber was the heart of a community dedicated to generating words. The scriptorium was the room in a Celtic monastery where skilled monks copied out the Bible by hand. You'd have heard the scratching of the quills, the rhythmic breathing of the scribes, the distant honking of a wild goose or the raucous call of a gull. From time to time, the low-pitched growl of mortar and pestle would reach your ears, as an apprentice ground out brightly colored powders destined to become paints.

The pace was slow and steady, the work unceasing during daylight hours, except for the times the whole enterprise ground to a halt for prayers. The brothers had little by way of possessions, but one thing they did have in abundance was time. The monks of Iona, Lindisfarne, and other remote communities were creating the rarest of treasures: folio-bound Bibles for a world hungry—then as now—for a word from the Lord.

It was exacting work. No room for error. Such errors as did occur were meticulously removed by scraping the sheepskin page with a razor-sharp knife.

None of those surviving pages are signed by the artist because it wasn't about the individual. Illuminating Scriptures was the work of the community. Apprentices succeeded masters as the decades rolled by, sometimes taking up the master's pen to continue the very page left incomplete at the prior evening's vespers.

Their work was about so much more than reproducing jet-black letters of the alphabet with flawless accuracy. The most skilled illuminators painted entire frontispiece pages, often embellishing a single letter. They embedded smaller artwork within the text. Occasionally, they added playful images—sacred doodling—in the margins.

The pinnacle of the Celtic illuminator's craft is the *Book of Kells*, named for Kells, Ireland, where the hefty leatherbound volume resided for a time before ending up in the Library of Trinity College Dublin. More than likely, the *Book of Kells* was created on the Isle of Iona, off the west coast of Scotland, then a notable center of piety and learning.

Those one-of-a-kind vellum manuscripts are worlds away from the mass-produced books we've known since the days of Herr Gutenberg. Iona seems even further removed from the softly glowing computer tablets we now hold in our hands, scrolling through electronic text. We can expeditiously export whatever we want with a few unskilled swipes. How the monks of the scriptorium would have marveled at such magic! Never has the word of God been more readily available than it is in our cloud-connected world.

Yet never has the word of God been more in need of loving, competent, and pastorally informed illumination. Those of us who have toiled through biblical exegesis courses may not easily recall how dense and impenetrable the Bible once seemed, as it does for so many of our listeners. Most long for deeper familiarity with the Good Book but don't know how to attain it. Well-chosen sermon illuminations shine light on the deep theological themes embedded in the sacred text. Such is the task of a preacher in a digital culture: no longer surrounding a single letter with intricate Celtic knotwork but rather contriving ways for Spirit-light to fall on a screen powered by a fading battery.

For many years, it's been fashionable to refer to the work of collecting and deploying secondary sermon material as illustration. But that's a word weighed down by certain deficiencies. *Illustration* calls to mind the full-page color plates publishers used to insert into hardbound novels. Old-time book illustrations were created by visual artists, known as illustrators, who typically worked from an early draft of the novel. Reflecting on the novelist's verbal description of the scene, illustrators recreated it in paints, in woodcuts, or on an engraving plate.

For generations, preachers understood the function of sermon illustrations in a similar way. After so many manuscript pages, they figured it was time to insert the obligatory illustration. That quotation or story provided a landing on the homiletical staircase, a little break for listeners to rest and regroup for the next flight of theology to come.

But that wasn't always the way. Illustrations are a fairly recent development in the history of homiletics. Eighteenth-century sermons by the likes of Jonathan Edwards and John Wesley are nearly devoid of illustrations. It was in the nineteenth and twentieth centuries that well-crafted illustrations became essential. Even so, many sermon illustrations from that era resemble those full-page plates dropped clumsily into the text. Such illustrations are in, but somehow not really of, the sermon.

This is despite the fact that churchgoers, on the way out the door, often praise illustrations as the most memorable part of the message. Perhaps it's their narrative form, or perhaps it's the right-brained processing they ignite, but illustrations have real staying power.

The second-class status of illustrations is even more astonishing considering the fact that it was Jesus's preferred mode of teaching (or, at least, the part of his teaching the Gospel writers remembered, which may say something in itself). Yes, we do have the aphorisms collection known as the Sermon on the Mount—more a compilation of memorable sayings than a transcript of any one talk—but it's Jesus's parables that Christians especially cherish.

So, let's not continue to talk of illustration, when illumination—enhancing the sermon's narrative flow rather than interrupting it—is more effective.

BORROWED LIGHT

The concept of borrowed light suggests how the best sermon illuminations work. Illuminations don't so much generate light as channel it. Such Christ-light as illumines the hearts of listeners doesn't originate with the preacher's carefully chosen stories. The stories merely spark it.

Homiletical scholar Thomas G. Long recalls a classic analogy explaining how the borrowed light within sermon illuminations work. Citing Charles Haddon Spurgeon—one of the few homileticians to write an entire book, *The Art of Illustration*, on this aspect of preaching—Long observes:

> Now and then, when homileticians of this period were searching for a way to explain this clarifying function of illustrations, they employed a revealing image (sort of an illustration about

> illustrations). Illustrations, they said, are "windows on the word." The sermon, they argued, is a house built with timbers of reason and logic, and illustrations are the windows bringing in the clear sunshine of comprehension. The nineteenth-century preacher and homiletician Charles Haddon Spurgeon employed this image when he advised his preaching students, "The chief reason for the construction of windows in a house is . . . to let in light. Parables, similes and metaphors have that effect; and hence we use them to illustrate our subject."[4]

There's something a little too regular and symmetrical, though, about conceiving preaching as a building trade. Just as architecture is both art and science, so, too, with preaching. In the homiletical house Spurgeon is envisioning, windows come along at regular intervals, every few yards. Countless sermon outlines over the years have followed a similar symmetrical design. The all-purpose plan of "three points and a poem" was the butt of many a seminary joke in my student days, and it may be still. In such a boilerplate blueprint, each point demands its own corresponding illumination, positioned as regularly as the windows of a clapboard farmhouse.

Borrowed light is a richer and more random concept. It's better suited for the growing number of digital natives among our listeners, who think less in terms of sequential arguments—ordered by a topic sentence and outline—and more in terms of hypertext. The preferred information-gathering style of today's listeners frees us to be more random and spontaneous than the ponderous sermon outlines of yore.

Old-school homiletics teachers held up a slightly less formal version of standard academic writing as a template for sermons. You needed an arresting illustration or joke to rouse your people from whatever torpor they might have drifted into, then a topic sentence

---

4 Thomas G. Long, *The Witness of Preaching*, 3rd ed. (Westminster John Knox, 2016), 227. Long is citing Charles Haddon Spurgeon in *Lectures to My Students* (Passmore & Alabaster, 1875), as quoted by John R. W. Stott, *Between Two Worlds: The Art of Preaching in the Twentieth Century* (Eerdmans, 1982), 240.

to define a human problem to be solved, then a brief exegesis to show how the day's Scripture addressed the problem, and then a sequence of outline points to lay out further implications and action steps. Each outline point merited its own illustration. The final point having been put to bed, it remained only to restate some variation of the topic sentence, then to offer something brief and memorable as a further flourish—a poem, a quotation, or a brief illustration—before uttering a closing prayer and transitioning into the next hymn.

Such a linear, sequential outline may still be standard in academic writing, but it's not how most people think. In response, some homiletics professors such as Paul Scott Wilson advise twenty-first-century preachers to avoid drawing attention to the outline structure of their sermons:

> Sermons are like stained glass windows: people look at the colored glass and see the light, not at the lead cames holding together the glass. Listeners generally are so busy trying to understand what the preacher is saying, and are so involved with the direction and thrust of the sermon at its surface level, that few are aware of its deep structure. Most people listen to a sermon simply for a way of understanding how God relates to the joy and sorrow of their own and others' lives. While they do not notice sermon structure, per se, they do notice if they leave church with more joy, hope, and promise than they had when they came. The preacher is probably the only one who will know that the sermon has a theological structure that assists the Holy Spirit in bringing forth hope.[5]

In preparing sermons, it's high time we broke out of the little boxes—be they the printers' color plates of yore or the window frames of Spurgeon's imagining. Unlike illustrations, illuminations aren't foreign objects embedded in theological text in order to adorn it.

5 Paul Scott Wilson, *The Four Pages of the Sermon: A Guide to Biblical Preaching* (Abingdon, 2018), 259.

They're organically part of the argument: at times giving it direction and shape but always shining light on gospel truth so others can see and understand it. Illumination is nothing less than preaching itself.

THUS SAYS THE LORD

The essential prelude to the illuminator's craft is the work of exegesis: a task akin to the ancient labor of grinding out pigments with mortar and pestle. Exegesis comes from a Greek word meaning "to lead out" or "to bring out." What's brought out, of course, is the text's larger meaning, informed by painstaking historical-critical study.

Exegesis is central to sermon preparation, but it's not our focus in this book. We're jumping in after you've completed the hard, foundational work of exegesis. You've studied the Scripture text in its original language or by comparing the best English translations. You've consulted learned commentaries for linguistic and historical insights. Most importantly, you've identified one or more theological terms arising from the text that seem to speak to the spiritual needs of your people in this place and time. This is where sermon illumination begins: just after you've distilled those all-important theological topic words out of the Scripture text and decided which ones will power your sermon.

For example, several theological themes arise from Jesus's parable of the good Samaritan (Luke 10:25–37). Compassion, kindness, hospitality, neighborliness, and anti-racism are a few. What about the terrified Elijah cowering in his cave, wallowing in his own despair until he hears God speaking in a sound of sheer silence (1 Kgs 19:9–17)? Courage, faith, perseverance, discernment, and vocation all come to mind. When Paul shares his memorable image of the body of Christ, composed of many members (1 Cor 12:12–26), church, unity, diversity, and conflict swiftly rise to the top. As the gobsmacked Mary Magdalene suddenly realizes that the gardener with whom she's speaking is no gardener at all

(John 20:11–18), resurrection, new life, faith, wonder, and witness could all be key talking points. Or some of them, anyway. One, perhaps two, of these rich concepts are more than enough for any single sermon (remember, there's always another Lord's Day). The topic words are primarily for you as you prepare your message. Topic words are your essential link between exegesis and experience. They're the coin of the realm, as far as sermon illumination is concerned.

On sweltering summer days in the 1960s, my brothers and I kept our ears alert for the jingling bells of the ice cream truck as it cruised our neighborhood. If we exercised all our persuasive powers, we could wheedle a dollar or two out of my mother for Popsicles. Standing outside the serving window of the ice cream truck, I was fascinated by the stainless-steel device the server wore on his belt—four shiny silos stocked with pennies, nickels, dimes, and quarters. That little machine had the power to swiftly break down our folding money into coins. Good sermons work like that, as they deftly refine high-value theological terms. You've got to break those big bills, making change for your listeners.

Exegesis is by no means all that's required to share the good news. Were that so, it would be enough to simply hand out Bible commentaries. No, what God's people require and cherish is someone they know—and who knows them—who's passionate about illuminating the text.

Let's also consider the work of inspiration. The word appears in 2 Timothy 3:16–17:

> All scripture is inspired by God and is useful for teaching, for reproof, for correction, and for training in righteousness, so that the person of God may be proficient, equipped for every good work.

The Scriptures the biblical author's writing about are of course the Hebrew Scriptures (the New Testament canon would not be formed for a couple more centuries). What's true of the Scriptures can also be said of faithful teaching that flows forth from them. To call a sermon inspired is the highest of praise.

The Hebrew prophets claim their own variety of inspiration. First Samuel 3 tells the story of the boy Samuel, repeatedly called by God in his dreams. After the high priest Eli confirms the boy's prophetic call, the biblical text says of him, "As Samuel grew up, the Lord was with him and let none of his words fall to the ground" (1 Sam 3:19). It's a typically earthy, concrete Hebrew metaphor, affirming that Samuel's prophetic utterances were divinely inspired.

Another indication of divine inspiration is the way Isaiah and so many other Hebrew prophets begin their teachings with the phrase "Thus says the Lord." Are any of us so bold as to begin our sermons that way? Were you to dispense with the usual pleasantries and open with those words, the phone of your supervising denominational official would swiftly light up with calls from overwrought congregants. Understandably so, because such boldness in preaching has long since gone out of fashion.

But is the church the better for it? Nearly two centuries ago, Ralph Waldo Emerson harshly lampooned a bookish, emotionally remote preacher of his acquaintance:

> I once heard a preacher who sorely tempted me to say, I would go to church no more. . . . A snowstorm was falling around us. The snowstorm was real; the preacher merely spectral; and the eye felt the sad contrast in looking at him, and then out of the window behind him, into the beautiful meteor of the snow. He had lived in vain. He had no one word intimating that he had laughed or wept, was married or in love, had been commended, or cheated, or chagrined. If he had ever lived and acted, we were none the wiser for it. The capital secret of his profession, namely, to convert life into truth, he had not learned.[6]

---

6 Ralph Waldo Emerson, "Divinity School Address," Harvard Divinity School, July 15, 1838, https://archive.vcu.edu/english/engweb/transcendentalism/authors/emerson/essays/dsa.html.

Whether or not we voice the actual words—and in our present authority-skeptical culture, we're better advised not to—"Thus says the Lord" is still the implicit promise behind Christian proclamation. Its promise of inspired preaching is why people come to church. They're seeking a word from the Lord.

The Greek word for inspiration is *theopneustos*, a compound term combining *theos*, or "God," with *pneuma*, or "spirit." *Pneuma*, of course, has an ordinary meaning of "breath," which is likewise true in the Hebrew language, where *ruach* means both "spirit" and "breath." Inspired speech, therefore, literally means "God-breathed."

That's a mighty high bar for any human communicator. A God-breathed sermon? *Really?*

Such a formulation didn't faze Heinrich Bullinger. He penned the Second Helvetic Confession of 1564, one of the notable historic confessions of the Reformed tradition. Bullinger famously—and audaciously—proclaims in a paragraph title: "The preaching of the Word of God *is* the Word of God."[7]

He doesn't mean it in the way you may think. Bullinger quickly adds the disclaimer that "the Word itself which is preached is to be regarded, not the minister that preaches." Inspired preaching, in his way of thinking, is an event that begins in the preacher's study but mysteriously takes shape somewhere between the breath leaving the preacher's lips and the sound of it being received in the congregation's ears and processed by their brains. The words of a sermon, hanging ever so briefly in the air, are far from holy writ. But the Holy Spirit is, according to Bullinger's way of thinking, uniquely and miraculously active in guiding those words to their target. Miraculously, the

---

7 The full text of that paragraph reads, "Wherefore when this Word of God is now preached in the church by preachers lawfully called, we believe that the very Word of God is proclaimed, and received by the faithful; and that neither any other Word of God is to be invented nor is to be expected from heaven: and that now the Word itself which is preached is to be regarded, not the minister that preaches; for even if he be evil and a sinner, nevertheless the Word of God remains still true and good." Presbyterian Church (U.S.A.), *Book of Confessions*, Second Helvetic Confession 5.004 (Office of the General Assembly, 2016), 77.

all-too-human words of the preacher serve as a humble container for God's living word, imparted to the congregation by the Holy Spirit.

You can look on the phrase "Thus says the Lord" as a sort of proffer. When you step into the pulpit, you're offering to your congregation the fruit of your own pursuit of God-sightings in daily life. The implicit promise, "Thus says the Lord," is still there, floating somewhere above the chandeliers like aromatic incense. You know it's there, and so do your people, even if you haven't explicitly claimed it.

But it's not all on you. Your people have a part to play in the preaching event. The preaching of the word of God can become the word of God only if the people believe it to be so. It's like the familiar call and response in the African American preaching tradition. The preacher proffers a phrase, then out of the assembly emerges "Amen" or any one of a number of similar vocalizations. The promise of "Thus says the Lord" is affirmed and fulfilled in such moments.

To claim that the preaching of the word of God *is* the word of God may sound extraordinary, even blasphemous. But in fact, nothing could be more ordinary. Divine inspiration is hardly unusual. We have a generous God who gifts preachers all over the planet with inspiration each Lord's Day. When the sermon preparation process breaks down—when an inspired insight fails to make it into a sermon—it's generally due to some shortcoming on our end. Such failures happen when we neglect to handle experiences of inspiration (those "that'll preach" moments that arise from our reading, our human interactions, and our devotional life) as a true curator of wonder would. We allow the feeling of wonder to dissipate. Unless we capture it in written form, keeping it in a safe place for later retrieval, we'll likely forget it altogether.

What I'm arguing here is that curating the raw illumination material for sermons is an essential part of the preaching event. Curation of this material is just as dependent on divine inspiration as assembling the words you'll eventually speak. It's a lifelong discipline, exercised through the weekly rhythm of sermon writing but unconstrained by it. It requires awareness, persistence, creativity, and openness to the Spirit's leading. It's good and holy work.

THE HOMILETICAL HELIX

There's another way of picturing the homiletical task. It's a model of what sermons typically look like. Unlike some other structural models, though—such as Eugene L. Lowry's *The Homiletical Plot*—this one is not so much a boilerplate visual outline as a way of imagining the conceptual interplay of Scripture text and topic.[8] This model recalls the double helix structure of DNA. Consider how biologists envision the structure of that complex molecule. It's like a ladder twisted into a spiral pattern (*helix* means "spiral"). What makes it a double helix is the fact that the twisted ladder has two legs.

There have long been two distinct approaches to sermon writing. A sermon may be textual—beginning from, and often deriving its structure from, the Scripture text. A subtype of textual sermon is the expository type, which typically offers a verse-by-verse commentary, although not every textual sermon is expository. Alternatively, a sermon may be topical: beginning from a theological or pastoral topic (often a human problem of some sort) and then reaching into Scripture to find and apply solutions to the problem.

Long have debates raged in homiletics classrooms about which starting point is best. Is it more faithful to begin with text or topic? Is a textual sermon inherently more biblical? Is a topical sermon more pastorally sensitive? Increasingly, these seem like the wrong questions to ask. What do such categories even mean, in a hypertext-loving world?

We can envision the two classic approaches, textual and topical, as the two legs of a ladder, which is fundamentally a two-dimensional structure. Twist the ladder into a helix pattern, though—venturing into a third dimension—and the connecting rungs no longer display the uniform right angles of the past. In this way of understanding a sermon's structure, it matters little whether text or topic comes first because the 3D helix shape assigns no priority to one ladder leg over the other. A helix has no front, back, or side. Because both legs are of equal importance, asking the question of which one takes precedence

8 Eugene L. Lowry, *The Homiletical Plot* (Westminster John Knox, 2000).

is nonsensical. A sermon may begin with scriptural exposition, or it may start out with a topic addressing individual or community need. Truly creative preachers are competent in both approaches. Whatever engages the congregation's imagination, whatever helps them follow the helix's successive twists and turns, is the correct jumping-off point.

A sermon envisioned as a double helix can be understood as both textual and topical. It matters little where in the helix structure one begins because the sermon's argument will soon begin moving back and forth between the spiraling legs. The metaphors, stories, poetry, and quotations that illuminate the sermon are like a ladder's rungs, bridging the two legs. Far from supplying mere ornaments or diversions, illuminations signal the shift from one leg of the twisted ladder to the other, providing the congregation with essential linkages between text and topic. Infused with the Holy Spirit, an inspired sermon's double helix hums with energy and glows with divine light. In such a sermon, old boundaries between form and content fade. Long insightfully suggests that the dividing line between form and content in sermons is no longer so easily distinguished:

> The picture we have in our heads is that of a preacher developing the content of a sermon and then hunting around for a suitable form, something like a shipping container, in which to box this content for delivery. In other words, content is the important stuff of the sermon; form is mere packaging, an afterthought. Outside of the mail room, however, the notion of a form as a package does not work. In artistic creations (and sermons are artistic creations of a sort), form and content cannot be easily distinguished.
>
> Instead of thinking of sermon form and content as separate realities, then, it is far better to speak of the form of the content. A sermon's form, although often largely unperceived by the hearers, provides shape and energy to the sermon and thus becomes itself a vital force in how a sermon makes meaning.

> Form is an essential part of a sermon's content and can itself support or undermine the communication of the gospel.[9]

Long quotes noted preacher Fred Craddock, who in his own preaching demonstrates a masterful use of stories:

> In good preaching what is referred to as illustrations are, in fact, stories or anecdotes which do not illustrate the point; rather they are the point. In other words, a story may carry in its bosom the whole message rather than the illumination of a message which had already been related in another but less clear way.[10]

In speaking of illumination rather than illustration, I'm reflecting this understanding of form and content as inextricably intertwined. We've seen how a medieval illuminated manuscript does embed images here and there, but in large part the artist's work consists of creatively rendering the Latin letters themselves. In our perception as readers, form and content are fused, rising up from the vellum page to become a thing of beauty.

One final aspect of the helix structure is worth pointing out: its spiral form. Think of a spiral staircase. Not only do its treads rotate around a central pole, but they also usher human climbers gradually upward. As a sermon progresses, it does more than merely hustle its listeners around a flat circle from Scripture to exegesis, to illumination, and to application. Gradually and repeatedly, it brings them back to a point directly over a place they've already been. In the most memorable sermons, listeners experience an aha of recognition as the preacher gives them a new metaphor that restates a thought they've already encountered but in a further uplifting way.

The Bible offers a model for such a meaning structure. Genesis 28:10–19 is the well-known tale of how the wandering Jacob takes a

---

9 Long, *The Witness of Preaching*, 136–37.

10 Fred B. Craddock, *Preaching* (Abingdon, 1985), 204.

stone for a pillow and falls asleep, then is captivated by a powerful dream. There's a central object in his dream, traditionally described in English translations as Jacob's ladder—although the New Revised Standard Version Updated Edition calls it "a stairway." That stairway is "set up on the earth, the top of it reaching to heaven, and the angels of God [are] ascending and descending on it" (28:12).

A great many biblical scholars have concluded that neither "ladder" nor "stairway" does the Hebrew word justice. The book of Genesis was likely compiled by exiled Jews in Babylon, who no doubt looked out their windows and saw, rising up from the very center of that foreign city, a towering temple known as a ziggurat. Around the edges of this squat tower were ramps or staircases leading upward. The ill-fated Tower of Babel in Genesis 11:1–9 likewise recalls the form of a ziggurat. The purpose of Babel's tower—as the priestly editors of Genesis describe it—was to allow their Babylonian captors to glorify themselves by constructing their own roadway to heaven. Jacob's imagined ziggurat, while similar in form, reflects no such hubris. His dream is not of a blasphemous human highway ramp but rather a pathway for the angels.

What if we were to conceive our double helix sermons as a similar pathway, along which—as the Holy Spirit permits—divine messengers may sometimes meet God's people where they are, coaxing them upward? Faithful seekers, like Jacob before them, may then marvel, "Surely the Lord is in this place—and I did not know it!" (28:16).

CHAPTER ONE

The Collector

Chasing the Shimmer

I grew up along the Jersey Shore and never tired of walking along the water's edge to see what treasures I might find glistening in the surf. The single, perfect, patterned seashell. The triangular fragment of smooth beach glass, deeply colored in green, brown, milky white or—most precious of all—blue. The rounded pebble, its marbled striations clearly displayed. The chunk of sea-soaked driftwood, its rich grain gleaming in the sun. The most alluring finds I used to pick up and take home with me. I washed the sand off in the bathroom sink and laid them out on my nightstand.

The next morning, I would awake to a surprise. My dried-out beachcombing treasures looked different. They lacked the transformative sheen of the sea. Clearly, they were the same items I'd picked up the day before, but it was as though life had gone out of them. They'd lost their shimmer.

It wasn't hard to restore the magical effect. I gave them a little tap-water bath, took them out in the sun, and the shimmer obligingly returned. But the effect was sadly temporary. It lasted only until the water evaporated.

The shimmer doesn't belong to the object itself, to the water, or even to the beaming sunlight. Somehow, it's a combination of them all, a whole greater than its parts. It's a wonder and a delight.

Part of it is the unabashed joy of discovery. The first glimpse of shimmering beach glass is unique. Even if the next day's tap-water bath approximates beachfront conditions, even if it catches the sun at exactly the same position and intensity, it's never so fascinating on the second or even third glance. If you could somehow point the wonder out to others, allowing them to make the same discovery in the object's natural habitat, their joy would rival yours.

Collecting material for sermon illumination is an essential part of the illuminator's art. We're all beachcombers as our eyes scan a page, a computer screen, or even the human drama transpiring ahead of us in the supermarket checkout line. What do we glimpse that's worth pocketing? What's better left behind? Will our pocket's contents still have the same allure a few hours later, as we spread out the daily catch and reexamine it?

Theologian Frederick Buechner has helped many of us in the preaching trade remain alert to wonders all around us. In this classic passage—written before the advent of word processors, when the persistent bell of a manual typewriter signaled the flow of creative thought—he captures the joy of finding the shimmer:

> We are all of us more mystics than we believe or choose to believe—life is complicated enough as it is, after all. We have seen more than we let on, even to ourselves. Through some moment of beauty or pain, some sudden turning of our lives, we catch glimmers at least of what the saints are blinded by; only then, unlike the saints, we tend to go on as though nothing has happened. To go on as though something has happened, even though we are not sure what it was or just where we are supposed to go with it, is to enter the dimension of life that religion is a word for.
>
> Some, of course, go to the typewriter. First the lump in the throat, the stranger's face unfurling like a flower, and then the clatter of the keys, the ting-a-ling of the right-hand margin. One thinks of Pascal sewing into his jacket, where after his death a

> servant found it, his "since about half past ten in the evening until about half past midnight. Fire. Certitude. Certitude. Feeling. Joy. Peace," stammering it out like a child because he had to. Fire, fire, and then the scratch of pen on paper. There are always some who have to set it down in black and white.[1]

That's us, who are brave or foolish enough to pursue the preaching trade. Most of us preach first to ourselves. Every word that makes its way into a sermon is filtered through our own spirituality. It's as much an expression of our own struggle for meaning as it is a retelling of the gospel's timeless message. Yet there's also the compulsion to share the shimmer with others.

In her Pulitzer Prize–winning nature memoir, *Pilgrim at Tinker Creek*, Annie Dillard recalls how, as a young girl growing up in the city, she pursued an unusual hobby. She used to hide pennies for strangers to find. Young Annie would nestle a shiny penny behind an exposed tree root or inside a sidewalk crack. Then she'd take a piece of chalk and draw large arrows directing pedestrians to the spot: SURPRISE AHEAD or MONEY THIS WAY. "I was greatly excited," she confesses, "at the thought of the first lucky passer-by who would receive in this way, regardless of merit, a free gift from the universe."[2]

It was a formative experience for an aspiring writer. In her adult life, Annie—a keen observer of the natural world who's been lauded as Thoreau's true heir—would achieve fame directing her readers to gleaming pennies scattered by the Creator. In her own words,

> There are lots of things to see, unwrapped gifts and free surprises. The world is fairly studded and strewn with pennies cast broadside from a generous hand. But—and this is the point—who gets excited by a mere penny? If you follow one arrow, if

---

1 Frederick Buechner, *A Room Called Remember: Uncollected Pieces* (HarperCollins, 1984), 152.

2 Annie Dillard, *Pilgrim at Tinker Creek* (Harper Perennial), 17.

> you crouch motionless on a bank to watch a tremulous ripple thrill on the water and are rewarded by the sight of a muskrat kit paddling from its den, will you count the sight a chip of copper only, and go your rueful way? It is dire poverty indeed when a person is so malnourished and fatigued as not to stop to pick up a penny. But if you cultivate a healthy poverty and simplicity, so that finding a penny will literally make your day, then, since the world is in fact planted in pennies, you have with your poverty bought a lifetime of days. It's that simple. What you see is what you get.[3]

Author Kathleen Norris, another keen literary observer, tells a similar tale. Curiously, it's also about the peculiar joy of finding pennies. Norris flags a certain oddness in the writer's penny-finding role—and the preacher's:

> I once observed a girl of about four years of age find a penny on the floor of a post office. "Look, mama, a penny," she said. Her mother, busy with the clerk at the window, mumbled an acknowledgment. I was surprised to see the girl put the penny back on the floor, in a different location. "Look, mama," she said again, "I found another one!" She kept it up until she had found five pennies, and each one of them new.
>
> The wisdom of that little child is difficult for grown-ups to retain. At the very least, we are expected to keep such foolish little games to ourselves. Mystics and poets do get to play, but although much lip service is paid to both traditions in our culture, it is largely condescension. No parent really wants his or her child to grow up and become a poet; no one in a religious house really wants to live next-door to a mystic. The task, and the joy, of writing for me is that I can play with the metaphors that God has placed in the world and present them to others

---

3 Dillard, *Pilgrim at Tinker Creek*, 17.

> in a way they will accept. My goal is to allow readers their own experience of whatever discovery I have made, so that it feels new to them, but also familiar, in that it is of a piece with their own experience. It is a form of serious play.[4]

The craft of collecting grist for the homiletical mill is, indeed, serious play. It's a strange pursuit. As in a quip variously attributed to Flannery O'Connor, G. K. Chesterton, and Dorothy Sayers but perhaps belonging to none of them, "You shall know the truth, and the truth shall make you odd." Not so many outside the guild will understand the peculiar joys of curation, but they do appreciate the finished result.

It's all about tapping the imagination. The Hebrew prophets were especially adept at holding up everyday objects that sparkle with divinity. As Eugene Peterson explains,

> The great masters of the imagination do not make things up out of thin air; they direct our attention to what is right before our eyes. They connect the visible and the invisible, the *this* with the *that*. They assist us in seeing what is around us all the time but which we regularly overlook. With their help, we see it not as commonplace but as awesome, not as banal but as wondrous. For this reason the imagination is one of the essential ministries in nurturing the life of faith. For faith is not a leap out of the everyday but a plunge into its depths.[5]

The prelude to great preaching is learning to see in this expectant, imaginative and ready-to-be-inspired way. Dillard speaks of sitting motionless on the bank of a woodland stream, but for preachers it may be reading a book, enjoying a video, wandering a museum, or entering into the sacred space of conversation. The shimmer may

---

4 Kathleen Norris, *The Quotidian Mysteries* (Paulist, 1998), 28–29.

5 Eugene H. Peterson, *Run with the Horses: The Quest for Life at Its Best* (Intervarsity, 2019), 72.

appear anywhere. Our business is to find it and start chalking arrows on the sidewalk.

THE LADDER OF ABSTRACTION

We all do it every day and every hour of our lives. But, like breathing, we're largely oblivious to it. It's the process known as abstraction. It's fundamental to our mental functioning—even to our survival. When curating sermon illuminations, though, abstraction is what you need to avoid.

Abstraction is an upward journey from concrete to conceptual, from particularity to principle. Our brains naturally combine unique, individual experiences with others to form a general class that, in turn, is combined with other perceptions to form ever-larger, more inclusive groupings.

We all learned how this works in elementary-school science class as we studied how biologists classify animals. First, they name an individual creature as belonging to a species. Then, they move up the taxonomic ladder to genus, then family, then order, then class, then phylum, and finally kingdom. With each step up the ladder, certain distinctive details fall away. Only common features survive. At the highest level—the animal kingdom—neither limbs nor scales nor beaks nor brains are obligatory. Earthworms coexist with elephants; paramecia, with porpoises.

Abstraction has its uses, but there are certain disadvantages that accompany the loss of detail. For example, to say that dogs make good pets is all but nonsensical. But to say that Labrador retrievers make good pets is something else altogether. But even that's a generalization. It doesn't always hold true. For those seeking a family dog, Labs' placid personalities make them a sought-after breed. But even among that loyal company of canines, there are curmudgeonly individuals whose unstable personalities bar them from home and hearth.

Theological education is among the most abstract of academic disciplines. Preachers displaying framed diplomas on their walls have spent years perfecting the art of writing academic papers that traffic in high-level abstractions such as justification, redemption, atonement, and grace. That A+ systematic theology paper could be worthy of publication in some learned journal, but it would be an absolute bust in any pulpit in the land. The art of illuminating a sermon demands a descent from the empyrean heights of abstraction into the everyday language and imagery of home and marketplace.

That sort of writing is a skill unrewarded in most seminary classrooms (preaching classes excepted). Aspiring preachers must unlearn certain writing skills laboriously acquired throughout their academic careers. Chief among them is the drift toward high-level abstraction. For most, this shift doesn't come easily. For some, it never does, to the detriment of their pulpit ministry.

BESSIE THE COW

Alfred Korzybski, the Polish philosopher and scientist who founded the discipline of general semantics, vividly warns of the pitfalls of abstraction with his famous dictum that the map is not the territory. Specifically, his warning goes like this: "A map is not the territory it represents, but, if correct, it has a similar structure to the territory, which accounts for its usefulness."[6] Whether unfolding an old-fashioned paper road map or mounting a smartphone on the car dashboard, we all know the experience of coming upon some unforeseen obstacle of which the map told us nothing. Maps abstract the reality of the terrain into a highly useful bird's-eye view, but the correspondence between map and territory is never exact.

6 Alfred Korzybski, *Science and Sanity: An Introduction to Non-Aristotelian Systems and General Semantics* (International Non-Aristotelian Publishing, 1933), 58.

Anyone who's read Lewis Carroll's *Alice in Wonderland* knows how that logician and mathematician delights in the absurd. In a lesser-known novel, *Sylvie and Bruno Concluded*, Carroll has a character playfully describe a map that has "the scale of a mile to the mile":[7]

> "What a useful thing a pocket-map is!" I remarked.
>
> "That's another thing we've learned from your Nation," said Mein Herr, "map-making. But we've carried it much further than you. What do you consider the largest map that would be really useful?"
>
> "About six inches to the mile."
>
> "Only six inches!" exclaimed Mein Herr. "We very soon got to six yards to the mile. Then we tried a hundred yards to the mile. And then came the grandest idea of all! We actually made a map of the country, on the scale of a mile to the mile!"
>
> "Have you used it much?" I enquired.
>
> "It has never been spread out, yet," said Mein Herr: "the farmers objected: they said it would cover the whole country, and shut out the sunlight! So we now use the country itself, as its own map, and I assure you it does nearly as well.[8]

Would that you—a preacher struggling to speak of the reality of God—could offer your listeners a theological map whose scale is a mile to the mile. But that's impossible. You've no choice but to use abstraction, although to use it effectively you must remain ever conscious of its limitations. For your sermons to communicate effectively, you must press your language as far down the ladder of abstraction as ever you can.

The most vivid expression of Korzybski's ladder of abstraction comes not from his own writings but from a book published by one of his disciples, S. I. Hayakawa. Hayakawa was a university

7 Lewis Carroll, *Sylvie and Bruno Concluded* (Macmillan, 1894), Chapter XI.

8 Carroll, *Sylvie and Bruno Concluded*, Chapter XI.

president who served California for a time as one of its US senators. In *Language in Thought and Action*, he describes a ladder of abstraction extending from the preverbal level of individual experience—a vision of a cow in a field—right up to abstract economic principles.[9]

At its most basic level, the cow is not a cow as we know it, but it "consists of atoms, electrons, etc., according to present-day scientific inference."[10] This Hayakawa calls "the process level."[11] If we could somehow take up a powerful electron microscope, zooming in to view the molecules that make up the cow, we would detect a whirling universe of subatomic particles that bears no resemblance to the bovine reality accessible to our five senses. But we're mostly unaware of the subatomic reality. Our brains automatically and unconsciously abstract that reality of the process cow, creating a mental image that necessarily leaves out many features of the underlying reality.

Reflecting on what we see with our ordinary vision, we name it Bessie, a name that is not the object in reality but merely stands in for it. Bessie is a particular individual that differs from other individuals having the same characteristics.

The next rung up the abstraction ladder is *cow*. That word denotes all the other individuals grazing in the field that resemble one another but that differ slightly. The pasture may contain many types of cows—Jerseys, Holsteins, and other varieties—but all demonstrate the reality we understand as cowness.

Moving further up that ladder—and taking in, now, other creatures on the farm—we come to the word *livestock*. Only the characteristics Bessie shares with pigs, chickens, goats, and so on are reflected in this term.

Next is farm assets. Bessie has a certain financial value that, along with tractors, silage, barns and fertilizer, can be added together to determine the farmer's net worth.

---

9 S. I. Hayakawa, *Language in Thought and Action* (Harcourt Brace Jovanovich, 1978), 82.

10 Hayakawa, *Language in Thought and Action*, 82.

11 Hayakawa, *Language in Thought and Action*, 82.

Next up the ladder is assets. Even more specific characteristics drop out with this label. We've now moved beyond the physical farm to lump Bessie in with less tangible treasures such as those preserved in bank accounts.

The highest level in this example is wealth, an extremely high level of abstraction. Almost all Bessie's distinctive characteristics have now fallen away. We're very far removed from the immediate, nonverbal sensory experience we first named. Too often, the practical effect of high-level abstraction—particularly in sermons—is obstruction.

CONCRETION IS INCARNATIONAL

The opposite of abstract is concrete. Although *abstraction* is a familiar word, concretion is less so. One dictionary defines *concretion* in this way: "a hard solid mass formed by the local accumulation of matter, especially within the body or within a mass of sediment." That hardly sounds appealing. But in the work of communicating ideas, concretion is what makes language sing.

Applying Hayakawa's Bessie-the-cow example, imagine you're taking a group of urban children on an outing to a farm. None of them have ever been to a farm before. They take it all in—the sights, the sounds, the pungent smells. You lead one of the kids up to a wire fence. On the other side stands Bessie, head down and contentedly grazing.

She's an impressive animal: large, powerfully built, and quite oblivious to the gaggle of schoolkids who've suddenly become part of her world. So very close to the fence is she that you could reach through and touch her flank. You invite a little girl to do just that. "Come on now," you say to her. "Would you like to reach through and pet Bessie?"

But what if you don't call her Bessie? You say, instead, "Come on now, put your hand through and pet this wealth." You would not be incorrect. Bessie (along with everything else in that agribusiness) is a small part of the farmer's wealth. But that's not why anyone takes city kids to visit farms.

You would be so very wrong in another sense. Your goal is not to give a small child an economics lesson. You want her to experience what life on a farm is like.

So, too, with God-talk in sermons. An important goal—perhaps the most important goal—is to help your people experience the divine. You don't do that with intricate theological language. That's a fool's errand. Few people have ever discovered God in the pages of a theology textbook (as important as such books are to plumbing the intellectual depths of religious experience). A great many more have found God in the pages of their Bible, particularly its vivid stories. A primary task of preaching is to invite listeners into deeper engagement with the Scriptures, where God-sightings await.

So as you decide which illuminations to use in the pulpit, it's vital that you remain conscious that you're always abstracting. Good illuminations demand that you reverse that tendency, moving down the ladder: choosing concrete, sensory language that invites listeners to imagine the same shimmer you once discovered. In doing so, you're not sharing exactly the same experience but something very similar to it.

Jesus himself is our model in this work of concretion. A great many of his teachings preserved in the Gospels are parables that live and move and have their being far down the abstraction ladder. Think of one of his most famous parables, the good Samaritan. It begins on the level of abstract theological discourse: a discussion of God's greatest commandment. Jesus and his scribal adversary agree on a stock response: "You shall love the Lord your God with all your heart, and with all your soul, and with all your strength, and with all your mind; and your neighbor as yourself" (Luke 10:27).

But then comes the comment that drives the conversation straight down the ladder of abstraction: "And who is my neighbor?"

Jesus could have responded with a rarefied theological argument about the true definition of neighbor, but he resists. Instead, he spins the tale of the unfortunate man who falls among thieves, whose life is preserved by the most unexpected of saviors.

Jesus's own life tracks a similar downward path. John's Gospel begins with the airiest of abstractions: "In the beginning was the Word, and the Word was with God, and the Word was God." But then, wonder of wonders, "the Word became flesh and lived among us, and we have seen his glory" (John 1:14).

Paul describes a similar trajectory in the famous kenosis passage of Philippians 2. Christ Jesus began "in the form of God" (What could be more abstract than that?), but he didn't remain on that level. Christ "emptied himself, taking the form of a slave, assuming human likeness." More than that, he "became obedient to the point of death—even death on a cross." Once Christ completed his downward journey, he soared back up the ladder: "God exalted him highly and gave him the name that is above every name" (Phil 2:5–11).

Preaching at its best—illumination that's conscious of abstraction and seeks to ground religious experience in concrete language—is kenotic and incarnational in this very way. My speech professor at Princeton Theological Seminary, Bill Beeners (echoing a statement attributed to poet T. S. Eliot) was fond of telling us how good literature turns blood into ink. To orally communicate such writing to our listeners, he went on, is a matter of turning ink back into blood.

The Things We Carry

> First Lieutenant Jimmy Cross carried letters from a girl named Martha, a junior at Mount Sebastian College in New Jersey. They were not love letters, but Lieutenant Cross was hoping, so he kept them folded in plastic at the bottom of his rucksack. In the late afternoon, after a day's march, he would dig his foxhole, wash his hands under a canteen, unwrap the letters, hold them with the tips of his fingers, and spend the last hour of light pretending.[12]

---

12 Tim O'Brien, *The Things They Carried* (Mariner Books, 2009), 1.

Those are the first lines of the remarkable 1988 novella of the Vietnam War, *The Things They Carried*, by Tim O'Brien. The author tells the story of a platoon of soldiers—ordinary grunts—as they go about the hard work of fighting a war no one knew how to fight. To tell his story, he uses detailed descriptions of the things they carried. Some are obvious:

> The things they carried were largely determined by necessity. Among the necessities or near-necessities were P-38 can openers, pocket knives, heat tabs, wrist watches, dog tags, mosquito repellent, chewing gum, candy, cigarettes, salt tablets, packets of Kool-Aid, lighters, matches, sewing kits, Military Payment Certificates, C rations, and two or three canteens of water. Together, these items weighed between fifteen and twenty pounds, depending upon a man's habits or rate of metabolism.[13]

Once the necessities are accounted for, O'Brien tells his readers of discretionary items like Lieutenant Cross's letters from Martha the college student, back home in New Jersey. Cross wasn't sure if she loved him, even though she signed her letters "Love, Martha." He hoped she did.

Ted Lavender was scared; he carried tranquilizers.

Norman Bowker carried a diary.

Ray Kiley carried comic books, brandy, and M&M's.

Kiowa, a devout Baptist, carried an illustrated New Testament presented to him by his father, back home on the reservation in Oklahoma. He also carried his grandfather's old hunting hatchet—a tomahawk, really—decorated with feathers.

Being soldiers, they carried not only weapons but also the heavy ammunition that went with them. "They carried all they could bear, and then some, including a silent awe for the terrible power of the things they carried."[14] There's a double meaning to the title, of course:

---

13 O'Brien, *The Things They Carried*, 1.

14 O'Brien, *The Things They Carried*, 1.

Not everything those soldiers carried through the rice paddies could be measured in pounds and ounces.

It's a brilliant literary move O'Brien makes. Somehow, his readers find out more about his characters from the objects they carry than if the author had described their personalities directly.

The novelist takes a deliberate journey down the ladder of abstraction. He could have simply told us, in general terms, about the personalities and predilections of these GIs. Instead, through artful use of detail, O'Brien upends their rucksacks and pours the contents out onto the ground. He *shows* us, leaving us to draw our own conclusions.

Mixing the Concrete

Before laborers pour concrete, they must first prepare it. For all but the smallest of jobs, they utilize a cement mixer: either a small model mounted on a wheeled cart or a large one on the back of a truck. Into the mixer goes the white, manufactured powder known as Portland cement, along with enough water to make a sort of paste. Next, they add materials known as aggregates: sand, gravel, or crushed stone. The drum of the cement mixer starts rotating and the aggregates tumble over each other, picking up cement paste as they go. Once the ingredients are uniformly distributed, the mix is ready to be poured into whatever mold or form has been prepared.

The concrete sidewalks many of us traverse each day are made up of more than just cement, despite the mistaken tendency to call them by that name. The bags of Portland cement that workers pour into the mixer account for no more than 10 to 15 percent of the slurry that's the final product. Water is another 15 or 20 percent, but aggregate is the largest ingredient by far. It's all in the mix.

The opposite of abstract is, as we've noted, concrete. Although the two meanings of that word—specificity and sidewalk—aren't closely related, there is a connection. The process of preparing concrete for a sidewalk can teach us something about the sort of language that provides a firm surface for a sermon's argument.

The word *abstract* comes from a Latin word meaning "to draw away, withdraw, or remove." Engaging in abstraction, you draw out the constituent parts of everyday reality into their elemental form. Korzybski, as we've seen, conceives it metaphorically as a journey up a ladder, but you could just as well see it as unweaving a tapestry into its constituent fibers.

Concrete, on the other hand, comes from another Latin word that means "to grow together." That's what grows inside a cement mixer: hence the name for the finished product.

Sermons, too, have their ingredients. Principally, these are exegesis, theology, and your parson's-eye view of the congregation's pastoral needs. It would be folly to literally build a cement sidewalk by laying bags of Portland cement end to end. Concrete is far better.

This is not to say there's no use for abstraction in preaching. On the contrary, identifying higher-level theological concepts is essential, especially when it comes to tagging database items with topic words. Those polysyllabic theological terms may seldom find their way into your sermon, but as topic words, they're the indispensable threads that lead you out of the database labyrinth, bearing just the right metaphor or story.

Your goal is to remain conscious of abstraction, being careful not to mistake abstract terms for the concrete experiences that invite your listeners in. By minimizing the use of abstract language from the pulpit, it's possible to produce a deeply theological sermon that never explicitly names the theological concept being taught.

And why is that a good thing? Here's why. The purpose of preaching is not to make congregants into junior theologians. Your purpose is to make disciples. As writers in the field of emotional intelligence are quick to point out, heart knowledge is equally as important as head language. At times, even more so. And it's concrete imagery that speaks to the heart.

Abstraction is vital to the process of sermon preparation. Gazing into your word-processor screen, you apply doctrinal lessons you learned in the classroom. You determine what the Scripture text says and identify one or more theological topics arising from it. Once you know which direction the sermon is going, though—once you know, generally, what sort of ingredients you'll be using—the sermon preparation has barely begun. You still need to add the grit and gravel of everyday life, in appropriate proportions, to create the product you'll deliver from the pulpit.

Concretion Strategies

Here are some reliable indicators that show you when your homiletical language is becoming more concrete.

- Use of an example. A classic move is to roll out the phrase "for example." This phrase, and others like it, signals a trip down the ladder of abstraction.
- Sensory language. Particularly in dealing with narrative scenarios, language that imaginatively engages the five senses is rarely wasted. It creates a "you were there" dynamic that helps listeners imagine what it felt like to live the biblical stories.
- Name individuals. Lose the hoary old "A little boy once said during a children's sermon" stories. Those vaguely attributed tales sounded stilted the first time they were told, and they don't improve in the retelling. If you can't name a particular individual for confidentiality reasons, then mention the place or time you happened to have that conversation (assuming such a conversation did indeed take place—truth matters in preaching, always). Political speechwriters know this concretion technique well. Instead of suggesting that their boss, the senator, talk abstractly about hard times the underemployed are going through, they supply a story about Suzanne, a single mother of two who works in a big-box store and whose boss never gives her enough working hours to qualify for benefits.

- Cite statistics. When appropriate, insert some carefully chosen statistics of recent vintage (but be careful not to overdo it with the numbers; they can quickly become overwhelming).
- Call to action. Move from the generic call to love your neighbor and toward a specific ask: Can you help out at the food pantry this Tuesday morning?

If all else fails, you can always resort to borrowing concrete illumination material from others, citing your sources in a way that makes it clear you didn't create it. It's more than acceptable to do so; no one expects you to exclusively present original research from the pulpit. Christian preachers have been borrowing from one another for as long as Christianity has existed. But if you borrow sermon material unethically, you'll encounter serious—possibly career-ending—pitfalls. You can read more about that in chapter 4.

PLACES THAT SHIMMER

In addition to attending to concretizations and abstractions, there are all sorts of likely places where you can collect pieces that shimmer for sermon illuminations. But these are not places to start looking late on a Saturday night. Illuminations that shimmer rarely present themselves on demand.

The best place to look is in your own reading. Sermons begin in the study. Good preachers are good readers—and not just readers of theology books. Literature and poetry are equally important sources. Keep in mind, though, that the canon of widely read novels is smaller now than it used to be. Gone are the days when the *New York Times* top-ten bestsellers were must-read items for many of our listeners, reliable fodder for dinner-party conversations. In nearly every case, you'll need to retell, at least in part, the scene or episode you're citing, because you can't be sure very many of your listeners will have read it.

Certain movies and streaming videos are becoming at least as broadly known as books, if not more so. Beware, though: Some of the most talked-about video content available through paid subscription services is not available to everyone. The Internet Movie Database (IMDb) site is the go-to place for plot synopses and quotations from films of every description. When citing lines of film dialogue, it helps not only to share the name of the character who said it but also the actor who played that character.

Online search engines such as Google are indispensable. The artificial intelligence (AI) powers of search engines are improving all the time. So, if you know you're looking for material on, say, learning to forgive yourself or discovering wonder, you're likely to find quotable material in short order. Be careful with search engines, though: They may take you to web pages that are poorly documented or offer false information. Some Google searches will include in their results short excerpts from Google Books, which can provide a line or two of text that's not only quotable, but also—because these are edited books—better documented than material from websites or social media posts.

Lectionary preachers in particular will find sermon resources sites and blogs such as Homiletics Online, Journey with Jesus, and Working Preacher to be excellent sources not only for exegesis but also for illumination material. The best of these sites provide not entire sermons but rather articles that suggest a general sermon direction along with supplementary exegetical and illumination material. As for the worst of such sites, their offerings are more like mass-produced motel-room decor than anything you're likely to see hanging in an art gallery.

Wikipedia, the crowdsourced online encyclopedia, is an indispensable source for illumination material of every kind. The crowdsourcing method of quality control (with legions of volunteer writers submitting material and editing the contributions of others) is surprisingly reliable—although, of course, for academic research a primary source is always preferable to its Wikipedia echo. Even for sermons, it's wise to check Wikipedia footnotes carefully to make sure the sources cited by the volunteer writers seem trustworthy. Wikipedia contains articles on most notable biblical passages as well as classic works of literature. It can be especially useful for content synopses. As for theological analyses, those can be all over the spectrum, depending on the orientation of individual writers. Caveat emptor on that.

Email newsletters—if they come from a source whose theological orientation you trust—can be invaluable. The "push" nature of these newsletters means that, at regular daily or weekly intervals, you receive materials you can conveniently cut and paste into your database for future use. The *Frederick Buechner Quote of the Day* and *Richard Rohr's Daily Meditation* are favorites of mine.

Digital newspapers help pastors fulfill Karl Barth's famous advice to preach with the Bible in one hand and the daily newspaper in the other. Although current news articles are of less-than-lasting relevance, op-ed and feature articles have a longer shelf life. Subscriptions to major newspapers like *The New York Times* and *The Washington Post* include the ability to search the paper's archives as well.

Social media can also be a source, although you need to handle this material with a great deal of caution, due to uncertain documentation. This is especially true of memes containing quotations by famous people. Generally, these list only the author's name, with no other information about what led the person to say it. It's astonishing how many quotation memes are complete fabrications. Even if the meme was posted by someone you personally know and trust, you have no way of knowing if that person verified the content or merely reposted it from someone else's feed. Generally, with social media quotations the best rule is to assume that the quotation is spurious until you've confirmed it using a documented source. Wikiquote, which operates on the same crowdsourced principle as Wikipedia, is an especially good way to source claims made in social media posts. Wikiquote often lists misattributed quotations as well as genuine ones, so you can use it to rule out spurious quotations as well as to confirm legitimate ones. Fact-checking sites such as Snopes are especially useful for flagging and ruling out urban legends.

Consider gathering a few trusted colleagues to form a preaching collective. Although such study groups are more common among lectionary preachers, it's also possible to do this with colleagues who organize their preaching topically. A typical online or in-person meeting format is to have one member of the group provide an exegetical paper as well as material for illuminating a sermon based on it. Group members independently write their own sermons, but each week's presenter gives everyone else a head start on the exegesis. Members should demand of each other high standards of documentation, footnoting sources they cite.

CHAPTER TWO

The Taxonomist

Tagging Your Finds

I was fortunate to spend my junior year of college imbibing the heady academic atmosphere of Oxford University. My ramblings around that medieval citadel of learning often led me to an imposing Victorian edifice known as the Pitt Rivers Museum.

It's a museum of ethnography—a fancy way of saying everything but the kitchen sink having to do with anthropology and human culture. In the mid-1970s, the Pitt Rivers resembled what you'd get if the British Empire held a yard sale. The collections were housed in a vast hall resembling a Victorian railway station. Its upper floors were wraparound balconies of ornate ironwork. It seemed like every inch of space, both on the main floor and the upper galleries, was taken up by old-fashioned, glass display cases. Inside the cases, you could view everything from Polynesian spears to Great Plains feather headdresses to shrunken heads.[1]

There was a vague sort of order to it all, but the overall ambience was dusty disarray. That suited me just fine because I'd come

---

1 The museum is now committed to confronting what it describes as "coloniality." A lengthy disclaimer on its web page laments the plundering of both sacred objects and human remains from colonized cultures, explaining that such formerly featured items have since been returned, as well they should be.

to love the Pitt Rivers as a place where you rummaged, wandering from display case to display case, seeing what treasures you might discover in nooks and crannies. But it could be a little hard at times to figure out what you were looking at because so many items were identified only by tiny cardboard tags dangling from pieces of string.

The second task of curating sermon illuminations is that of the taxonomist, who selects topic words to identify and later retrieve them. But those dusty display cases are emblematic of what the tagging task within illumination curation is not meant to be. If, over the course of many years in the pulpit, you assemble a burgeoning collection of stories, quotations, and other ephemera, you must have some way of drilling down within that collection to rapidly uncover what you need. Predictably, some items from only a few years back will prove to be outdated. They're best left alone or even deleted.

THE WAND FINDS THE WIZARD

Featured prominently in J. K. Rowling's Harry Potter novels is Ollivander's Shop—makers of fine wands since 382 BCE—located in the ephemeral Diagon Alley. It's the place young Hogwarts students go to find the unique wand they'll carry for life. Ollivander's is the picture of dusty disarray: a tiny, hole-in-the-wall emporium with floor-to-ceiling shelves. Wand seekers rely on Mr. Ollivander's incredible memory to locate exactly the right one. But it's not so much they who find their wand: The wand finds the wizard.

For Harry, it's not an easy process. He tries and discards one wand after another, but the patient Ollivander is relentlessly cheerful. He's midwifed many a frustrating wand search in his time:

> "Tricky customer, eh? Not to worry, we'll find the perfect match here somewhere—I wonder, now—yes, why not—unusual combination—holly and phoenix feather, eleven inches, nice and supple."

> Harry took the wand. He felt a certain warmth in his fingers. He raised the wand above his head, brought it swishing down through the dusty air and a stream of red and gold sparks shot from the end like a firework, throwing dancing spots of light on to the walls. Hagrid whooped and clapped and Mr. Ollivander cried, "Oh, bravo! Yes, indeed, oh, very good."[2]

"That'll preach," we mutter to ourselves, the moment the right story or metaphor presents itself. It's what we say when the wand finds us. If you've properly tagged your discoveries and stored them in a database, you won't need Ollivander's uncanny gift of discernment to find them later.

Ollivander's wand emporium is anything but a model of efficient organization. But that's hardly necessary in his case. Ollivander has something going for him that we don't: magic. Who needs an efficient filing system when you know that, in the end, the wand finds the wizard?

Would that the same were true of sermon material! We've all marveled when the perfect anecdote appears unbidden, but who can count on such magic repeating itself? It's a good thing there's a homiletical hack, a way to hedge our bets. The solution is to create a database and fill it over time. It's a solution unavailable—and undreamed of—for earlier generations of preachers, for whom a commodious file cabinet was the height of technology.

The purpose of an illuminations database is to preserve the shimmer. Creative ideas for sermons are hardly in short supply, but they're ephemeral. They've got an annoying way of giving your consciousness the slip shortly after they wink at you, as more recent memories edge them out. Those inspirations still reside somewhere in your brain, but they swiftly recede into the background. A great many of them disappear in the cerebral shadows.

---

2 J. K. Rowling, *Harry Potter and the Sorcerer's Stone* (Scholastic, 1998), 84–85.

Think of your illuminations database as a map of your own mind—or, at least, the part of your mind whose job it is to think creatively. When a topic search obligingly summons up a sermon idea from half a year ago, there's a joyful recognition: "Oh yes, I remember that now!" Lo and behold, after a splash of water, the shimmer's still there.

LESSONS FROM THE *BEAGLE*

The key to retrieving just the right sermon illumination is a skill that was well known to nineteenth-century naturalists like Charles Darwin. The skill is taxonomy—the science of organizing and classifying discoveries, primarily from the natural world. When, following God's command, Adam names the animals in Genesis 2:19–20, he becomes the very first taxonomist. In a sense, Darwin was Adam's heir, taking that work to new heights.

Darwin took his taxonomy skills with him when, in 1831, he boarded the Royal Navy's HMS *Beagle* for what would become a five-year journey around the world. Onboard, he was a supernumerary (a self-funded gentleman passenger rather than a member of the crew). The *Beagle*'s commission was to survey the coastline of South America, with the goal of updating Royal Navy hydrographic charts—the maps captains rely on to avoid submerged rocks and reefs. Scientific organizations like the Royal Society had convinced the Admiralty to make room on such expeditions for naturalists like Darwin, as a way of advancing human knowledge.

The slow pace of ocean voyages in the age of sail allowed ample time for Darwin to disembark at various points, while navy officers took their soundings and drew detailed maps of the coastline. His job was to make scientific observations and collect plant and animal specimens for transport home. Darwin observed and recorded data on a variety of species. Most significant for the future of science, he took a particular interest in several new species of finch he discovered on the Galápagos Islands.

Darwin noticed the Galápagos finches were similar to those he'd catalogued on the South American mainland but with small variations in beak size and shape. He marveled at how well adapted the beaks of Galápagos finches were to particular types of food, whether seeds or insects. Darwin speculated that, over many generations, the various island species had evolved from a single mainland species. He called this evolutionary process "natural selection."

This was a new way of looking at the natural world. Until Darwin, a great many European scientists—naively presuming the Genesis creation stories were scientifically precise—assumed the number of animal species was finite and unchanging. They further assumed God must have gifted each species, including examples like the various Galápagos finches, with unique attributes that allow each subspecies to thrive in its particular ecological niche. Because of his meticulous observation of small differences between avian species, Darwin amassed evidence for the gradual evolution of species over a time frame vastly longer than the biblical seven days.

What allowed Darwin to draw these world-shaking conclusions was his skill as a taxonomist, a namer of creatures. Observing common characteristics among the species, he arranged newly discovered creatures, both plant and animal, according to broader categories such as phylum, class, order, family, and genus.

Ministry—particularly preaching ministry—is the last great generalist vocation. I learned this years ago when I served as director of admissions at the University of Dubuque Theological Seminary in Iowa. The seminary dean, Arlo Duba, informed me that applications from undergraduate religion majors were not particularly favored. The entire seminary program was itself a religion major, but what the faculty really wanted was students who had a broad grounding in the liberal arts. Even scientific or technical majors, like engineering, nursing, or computer science, made the grade as long as the applicant had taken a sufficient number of liberal arts electives.

In this age of hyperspecialization, if you're so bold as to undertake the work of sermon illumination, you need to be something of a polymath and be willing to become an expert taxonomist. You have to know the right topic words for naming those metaphors, stories, poetry, and quotations you've discovered, preserving them for future use.

The most effective preachers are not narrowly focused biblical studies specialists. If you're going to preach and do it well, you have to know a little about a lot. You have to read widely. Not just Bible commentaries but literature, history, current events, the arts, and whatever your people are reading and experiencing. This is as it should be, because your congregation bears little resemblance to that narrow segment of humanity to whom you preached your seminary chapel sermons. Unless it's very unusual, your congregation is far more diverse, composed of people from every walk of life. To touch them where they live, you must—with the broad interests of an old-time naturalist—gather diverse units of literary material. You'll name each one, with a taxonomist's precision, so you can retrieve them when the time is right.

LABYRINTHS AND COLD FRAMES

The Greek myth of Theseus has at its center the remarkable contrivance known as the Labyrinth. Unlike the two-dimensional walking labyrinths commonly used as an aid to prayer, the original Labyrinth was an impossibly difficult maze with high walls and unpredictable twists and turns. At the center of the Labyrinth resided the minotaur, a fearsome beast with a man's body and a bull's head.

King Minos of Crete had installed the monster there as a way of punishing his defeated rivals, the Athenians. According to the harsh terms of the peace treaty, every nine years the Athenians had to offer up seven young men and seven young women to be driven into the maze as minotaur fodder.

Theseus, the Athenian hero, goes undercover as one of the human sacrifices. He smuggles a sword in with him. But slaying the beast, as it turns out, is the least of his problems. The hero still has to find his way back out of the enchanted maze.

Fortunately, the king's daughter Ariadne—who's fallen in love with the dishy Theseus—has given him a hot tip: Carry a spool of thread with you, unwinding it as you go. As the triumphant hero holds the minotaur's head in one hand, he uses the other to trace the string back through the darkness to freedom.

A database facilitates just that sort of journey back. Entering its maze to deposit a new quotation or story, you're prompted to attach a string (topic words or other identifiers) so you can retrieve it later.

Even with a guiding string to help you navigate your collection, many of the best illuminations require a gestation period. You read or experience something and say to yourself, "This'll preach," but you're not sure exactly how or when. No problem. Just file it away, and one of the topic words you've given it will lead you back eventually.

Some sermons have a blessedly short gestation period. A new idea may spring unexpectedly to life and suitable illuminations present themselves unbidden. But sooner or later, beset by the relentless and varied demands of ministry, eager but unprepared preachers hit a wall. The homiletical cupboard is bare. This is when a cold frame pays big dividends.

Gardeners in northern latitudes are familiar with an ingenious device known as a cold frame. It's a minigreenhouse used in early spring, when snow still flecks the ground, to jump-start the growing season. The moniker's a bit misleading because the purpose of a cold frame is not to refrigerate seedlings but to keep them warm when the outside air is still cold. Gardeners plant seeds in small pots under the cold frame weeks before the growing season has begun. Later, once the garden soil has grown warm enough for survival, they transplant the seedlings. No tomatoes—none worth speaking about, anyway—would ever grow from seed in Montana, Minnesota, or Maine were it not for cold frames.

As a preacher, if you've taken a cold-frame view rather than approaching sermon preparation as a series of discrete, week-long units, you'll be in much better shape when crunch time inevitably arrives. If you've been nestling sermon seeds into pots of black soil under that cold frame, you'll find you have numerous options to choose from. Even if you haven't been following such an approach, don't despair. There's no time like the present to begin it.

You'll soon learn to plant more seeds in the cold frame than you'll ever need. A few will never germinate. Some seedlings will poke their impertinent heads above the soil but fail to thrive. But there will always be some ready for transplanting just when they're needed.

To do this sort of work, you have to think long term. No gardener has ever successfully used a cold frame without envisioning the entire growing season. In a similar way, in any given week you can be working on multiple sermons, saving your work in the cold frame that is your filing system.

A gardener's cold frame is a low structure constructed out of lumber and window glass, whose transparent roof you can lift up when you need to water the seedlings. If you're a preacher, you need something different. You need a database.

FROM BOTTOM DRAWER TO DATABASE

Years before home computers existed, I learned the value of collecting sermon material from one of my professors at Princeton Theological Seminary, Ernest T. Campbell. Ernie had recently retired as pastor of the Riverside Church in New York City. I no longer recall the name of his course or what was on his book list, with two exceptions. Both were unusual things to find among the piles of weighty textbooks in the seminary's Theological Book Agency.

One was a cheap paperback version of Annie Dillard's *Pilgrim at Tinker Creek*—the intricate and moving journal of nature observations I mentioned in chapter 1. The second was a tiny blank notebook, sturdily bound in the manner of a hardcover book. It was small and thin enough to fit into a shirt pocket or purse. Ernie emphatically demanded that we all purchase that particular notebook and none other. He got some groans from the class over that requirement, because the blank book's sturdy, stitched binding made it pricey.

A major course assignment was to carry those tiny notebooks around for the entire semester, preserving material that could be useful in sermons. Ernie made it clear that anything was fair game: not only things we were hearing in lectures but also excerpts from books (especially novels), random anecdotes from *The New York Times*, even fragments of dining-hall conversations.

It was nothing less than a journal of intellectual discovery. As the young Annie Dillard had once, in Godlike fashion, scattered pennies in sidewalk cracks, Ernie sought to convince us we could find divine inspiration for preaching all around us—if only we aligned our hearts to receive it. It was low-hanging fruit we could easily snatch. All we had to do was pay attention.

Ernie was serious about the black notebook being a course requirement. We had to hand it over on the last day of class for him to examine and grade. No exceptions. What he was grading was not so much the content we'd assembled as the personal discipline we'd practiced over the entire semester. He was teaching us to build a kind of theological muscle memory, training us to keenly observe and diligently record the quirks and wonders of God's world.

Ernie admitted he wasn't so systematic about filing. Some pre-internet preachers maintained index-card files of illustrations, complete with cross-references, but he wasn't one of them. Once Ernie filled up a little black book, he simply moved on to another. He told us he'd filled dozens of them over the years, but he rarely looked back any further than the most recent one. Most everything older than that, he explained, had grown stale for him. As for longer texts, like newspaper and magazine articles, he simply clipped them and dropped them into the bottom drawer of his desk. When the drawer filled up, he discarded the items on the bottom to make more room.

Late 1970s filing technology was analog. The time demands of building an efficient, paper-based filing system were prohibitive for pastors whose job descriptions required them to do much of anything other than preaching. Ernie's method of dropping everything into the bottom drawer was appropriate technology for those days.

Of course, we no longer live in such a world. We carry smartphones whose processing power vastly exceeds that of the Apollo moon lander and that are, coincidentally, about the same dimensions as Ernie's pocket notebook. We're rarely far away from tablets and laptops that effortlessly cut and paste text, storing it in the cloud. As long as we efficiently tag our discoveries so we can find them later, their shelf life increases exponentially. Yes, training our theological muscle memory to discover sermon seeds is still just as vital, but now we have a better place to store those seeds: a database.

I'm not going to recommend a particular database program. That's an individual choice. There are many software options out there—some of which could become obsolete in time, so beware of that potential pitfall. You absolutely have to think long term when making this choice, because switching from one program to another mid-career is not something you ever want to do. So, invest a little money now in a proven product that's likely to be available decades into the future.

It's also important to make sure the program is infinitely expandable and won't slow down your computer once the content grows beyond a certain size. Like Ernie Campbell throwing out the bottom tier of papers stacked in his bottom drawer, I agree it's not a good use of time to laboriously cull obsolete items one by one. But with a database, you don't have to. You can leave older material right where it is, because you'll never run out of room. A good database program has more capacity than anyone could fill in a lifetime. When I perform a search, I simply start reading the most recent entries under my chosen topic word (or other identifier) and work backward in time until I find something that shimmers.

More than thirty years ago, I started using a sermon illustrations database program constructed in Microsoft Access by a fellow pastor. He made the program available free on the internet and still does.[3] I haven't regretted my choice, although I have repurposed a few of the fields. Were I starting out today, I might use a free-form note-taking program like Evernote that, while not a classically designed database, allows for hashtagging entries by topic keywords. It also allows for easy cutting-and-pasting of entire web pages and screenshots rather than plain text. While it can be useful to save URLs (web addresses) along with the content, beware of saving the URLs alone. Much of the internet is ephemeral. Web pages can and do go away, and a URL that takes you to the dreaded "file not found" notice is all but useless.

Plan on tagging items using multiple topic keywords. That functionality is essential, because most items can apply to more than one topic. Be sure your program also offers options for tagging by source name, author's name, and Scripture citation. You'll use those types of search terms less often than topic words, but they're still handy. If you're a lectionary preacher, it can be useful to file certain items according to Sundays of the liturgical year. You'll probably find, though, that topic words will be your go-to choice in most instances.

Your database is where your preaching intersects with your theology. A great many of your most useful topic words will be theological terms. Although twenty-dollar words should be used sparingly in preaching—a sermon is not a theology lecture, after all—they're the most efficient way for your past self (the person who filed the database entry) to speak with your present self. A considerable part of the preacher's art is finding ways to teach complex theological concepts without inflicting weighty academic terms on disciples who haven't known the luxury of graduate theological education. This is not to demean your listeners' intelligence, but there's simply no reason to

---

3 The database I use is still available as a free download at http://www.holwick.com, but you need to buy and install Microsoft Access in order to run it. As of this writing, Rev. David Holwick, its creator, is still maintaining this web page as a gift to the preaching universe. He makes it available both with and without sermon illustrations; it was my personal choice to download the empty database and build its content using only my own material.

mention theodicy as you address the intractable problem of why bad things happen to good people or ecumenism as you ponder the thorny question of why Christians just can't seem to get along. But such words are ideal search terms for your database.

Whether you choose a tags-based note-taking program like Evernote or a more traditional database like Microsoft Access, it's important to settle on consistent nomenclature early on. When you cite Scripture passages, either use a standard table of abbreviations or simply write out the full name of the biblical book. Are Roman or Arabic numerals best for books like First and Second Kings or First and Second Corinthians? It doesn't matter. You decide, as long as your data-entry conventions are consistent.

If you're filing material according to Sundays of the liturgical year, you'll likewise need to follow a standard format. I use a simple system that keeps citations short: BLent4, for example, stands for Year B, Fourth Sunday in Lent. My database offers a parallel section for filing the full text of past sermons: I use the liturgical year tags more often for recalling whole sermons than I do for individual items.

As the years go by and your database grows, you'll also appreciate having some way to record your usage history. The longer you stay with a given congregation, the more important this becomes. I've always had an aversion to repeating myself: Not only is it less interesting for me to revisit familiar territory, but it's also surprising how long some listeners' memories can be.

Here are some useful fields for a classic database (or hashtag words for a note-taking program):

- Topic words—must allow for multiple options (tag example: #topicGrace)
- Title—your thumbnail description of each item, a time-saver as you scroll through multiple entries
- Author (tag example: #authorBuechnerFrederick)
- Source
- Scripture text (tag example: #1Cor13:1)

- Date(s) previously used (tag example: #20240714, for July 14, 2024)
- The URL of the web page where you found it

A similar taxonomy can be used for your own sermon manuscripts or outlines:

- Topic words (tag example: #topicGrace)
- Title
- Location preached
- Date preached (tag example: #20240714, for July 14, 2024)
- Scripture text (tag example: #1Cor13:1)
- Lectionary Sunday designation (tag example: #BLent4)

CHAPTER THREE

The Librarian

Tapping Your Collection

Reference librarians are adept at helping researchers locate the material they need. In curating sermon illustrations, you have to be your own librarian as you retrieve materials from your database. Three decisions serve to narrow the field before you start retrieving items from your archive to use in a sermon. These are choosing a text, topic, and provisional title.

Occasionally, a sermon may have more than one biblical text—particularly if one text opens up the meaning of another—but a single text is the norm.[1] A text may be as brief as a single verse or even a fragment of a verse. Rarely is it longer than two or three verses.

In some faith traditions, the sermon text is a portion of one of the day's Scripture readings. Lifting a verse or two out of the larger passage contributes mightily to a sermon's focus. To identify a sermon text in this way doesn't mean you're forsaking the rest of the

---

1 If you're a lectionary preacher, it's generally best to resist the temptation to preach on more than one of the lectionary texts for a given Sunday. Yes, sometimes the lectionary designers chose specific texts to complement each other, but that's not always the case. Even if there is a theological common thread, it may not be the same theme you've chosen to lift up, based on your primary text. One Scripture text is more than enough for most congregants, who are far less curious about the internal workings of the lectionary than you are.

pericope. Your choice of text merely pounds a stake into the ground wherever you've discovered the shimmer.

A sermon's topic is basically what it's about. It's what you're trying to say, summed up in a single sentence.[2] The topic is the sermon's purpose: the message it communicates, the outcome you hope to see in your listeners' lives. It's the takeaway.

Text and topic have a role to play in the double helix sermon model set forth in the introduction. Recall that the helix has two spiraling legs. These correspond to text and topic. It matters not which strand of the helix you choose as your starting point. Some sermons will begin with the text, moving outward to address a topic of human need. Others begin with the need, then look to the Scriptures for guidance in addressing it. Still others shuttle back and forth between the two.

The illuminations are the ladder rungs connecting text and topic at various points along the way. In one sense, they function as tie-rods, maintaining tension between text and topic, bending each leg of the ladder in such a way that it engages in a spiraling dance with the other. In another sense, they serve as bridges, allowing listeners to make the transition back and forth from text to topic or vice versa.

The third *t* is title. A sermon's title usually has some obvious relation to its topic sentence. It may be a concise summation of the topic sentence, or it may be one aspect of it, lifted out from the rest because of its power to engage imagination. Occasionally, it may arise out of the other leg of the helix, the Scripture text—although in that case, it's wise to make sure it relates somehow to the topic as well, because you can never assume your listeners are as interested in the Scriptures, in and of themselves, as they are in seeing how the Scriptures speak to their lives.

The title serves listeners as a way of inviting their attention and it serves you as a tag for identifying the sermon in the future. At this

2 In the world of homiletics, there's some ambiguity about the meaning of the word *topic*. To some, a sermon topic is the same as its title. I'm using the word *topic* a little more broadly. It's the topic sentence of the sermon: similar in meaning to the title but not identical to it.

retrieval stage, all titles are provisional. It's not unusual to change the title, based on new ideas that emerge.

The writing process begins the moment text, topic, and provisional title have been determined, even if this is weeks or months in advance. I've known colleagues who plan their preaching a year in advance, going off on retreat to provisionally choose upcoming texts, topics, and titles. Others do that several times a year, nailing down entire seasons of the liturgical year. At a bare minimum, you can decide on text, topic, and title around ten days ahead of time. That interval provides enough time to publish the Scripture reading and title of the upcoming sermon in the church's weekly newsletter, website, and worship bulletin. In many congregations, church musicians may require a longer interval, to allow time for choosing and rehearsing special music. Your mileage may vary, in other words.

The best sermons aren't written in a few hours or even a single day. That's because the creative process is about far more than the final step of putting words on paper or into the tablet. The retrieval period is a time not only for scouring your database for material but also for engaging in prayer and reflection. Some key insights arise subconsciously, in the form of thoughts captured by the brain's peripheral vision, or even in dreams. All this takes time.

From the moment the text presents itself, a period of creative brooding commences. Through prayer, reflection, and silence, you discern what you believe the Lord is saying to and for your particular congregation. It can be helpful to do some basic exegesis and consult a few trusted Bible commentaries at this stage, but far more important is the work you do in discerning what you believe God's saying to the people. You're qualified to do this because you know something professional exegetes—not to mention AI writing programs—do not: You know your people and their specific needs. You exegete the congregation just as you exegete the text.

This period of contemplative reflection is an opportunity to revisit your decisions about text, topic, and provisional title. More often than not, these continue to shape the sermon, although occasionally the Spirit leads in a different direction. When that happens, it's time to abandon the prior plan without a second thought and seek out whatever shimmers.

Episcopal priest Barbara Brown Taylor describes how such a period of creative brooding is essential to the illumination process:

> It is time to tuck the text into the pocket of my heart and walk around with it inside of me. It is time to turn its words and images loose on the events of my everyday life and see how they mix. It is time to daydream, whittle, whistle, pray. This is the gestation period of a sermon, and it cannot be rushed. It is a time of patient and impatient waiting for the stirring of the Holy Spirit, that bright bird upon whose brooding the sermon depends. Over and over again I check the nest of my notes and outlines, searching through them for some sign of life. I scan the text one more time and all of a sudden there is an egg in plain view, something where there had been nothing just a moment before, and the sermon is born. . . . It is as hard for a preacher to say how this is done as it is for a painter to say how a tree takes shape on a canvas. Do the leaves come first or the branches? What combination of yellow and blue makes such a bright green? How do you make it look so real? All the parts of preaching can be taught: exegesis, language, metaphor, development, delivery. What is hard to teach is how to put them all together, so that what is true is also beautiful, and evocative, and alive.[3]

OLD MEN WILL DREAM DREAMS

Here's a lesson I've learned only in recent years. I wish I'd trusted dreams more, earlier in my ministry. For most of my active ministry, I was moderately—sometimes severely—sleep deprived. Partly this was due to obstructive sleep apnea, a medical condition now

3 Barbara Brown Taylor, *The Preaching Life* (Cowley, 1993), 81–83.

corrected through nightly use of a BiPAP machine. But the greater part of my sleep deprivation was the result of overwork: particularly in the late-night hours, when I would return to the computer in a mostly vain attempt to finish the work of the day before stumbling off to bed exhausted.

In retirement, I've rediscovered something I'd known from an early age but had largely forgotten: the essential link between dreams and creativity. Now that my sleep schedule has returned to normal, I've come to appreciate this anew.

The last hour or so of a healthy sleep cycle is a time when dreams match up, in fascinating ways, with tasks that are foremost in our minds. If I'm engaged in an ongoing writing project, stories and metaphors float into my consciousness in those last moments of sleep—but only briefly. I keep my smartphone on my nightstand, and should I awake with the memory of such dreamwork fresh in my mind, I use a simple note-taking app to quickly capture a fleeting metaphor or turn of phrase. These rough notes are like the line on a fishing pole, enabling me to reel in thoughts that might otherwise disappear into the night.

I've found I can often do this several times in the course of my last hour or so of sleep. Once I've offloaded the compelling thought that woke me up, I no longer worry about forgetting it. I can put my head back on the pillow and again set my dreams adrift. More often than not, further insights will awaken me, and I repeat the procedure of writing them down. This is one more reason why it's not wise to begin writing a sermon on Saturday evening. Creativity—dream inspired or otherwise—takes time.

Poet Julia Ward Howe used this technique during the Civil War to write her famous poem that became the beloved "Battle Hymn of the Republic." Howe had journeyed with her husband to Washington, DC, with the goal of doing something to support the Union troops encamped around the city. Traveling back from one of these excursions, she and her husband found themselves among soldiers lustily singing "John Brown's body lies a-moldering in the grave, but his soul goes marching on." The popular ditty was eminently singable, but the words left something to be desired. A friend challenged her to write a more uplifting lyric.

The next morning, Howe awoke from a sound sleep with the tune of "John Brown's Body" echoing in her mind. As she later described it,

> I awoke in the gray of the morning twilight; and as I lay waiting for the dawn, the long lines of the desired poem began to twine themselves in my mind. Having thought out all the stanzas, I said to myself, "I must get up and write these verses down, lest I fall asleep again and forget them." So, with a sudden effort, I sprang out of bed, and found in the dimness an old stump of a pen, which I remembered to have used the day before. I scrawled the verses almost without looking at the paper.[4]

The resulting product was still not ready for prime time. Reflecting back on past experiences of "attacks of versification [that] had visited me in the night," Howe describes how the words she'd frantically penned in semidarkness were nearly unreadable the next morning: "I was always obliged to decipher my scrawl before another night intervened, as it was legible only while the matter was fresh in my mind."

The Sufi poet Rumi had much the same idea about this pregnant interlude between sleep and wakefulness when he advised spiritual seekers: "The breezes at dawn have secrets to tell you. Don't go back to sleep."

Dreams are vital to retrieving material we know but aren't consciously aware that we know. Think of them as access points to the free-flowing river of the subconscious. Beneath the solid pavement of your life runs a mighty river, coursing through a vast underground aqueduct. Your dreams allow you to ride its waters but only briefly. You spend most of your hours toiling on the mean streets above this river, scarcely aware of its existence. Here and there are maintenance holes that go through to the subterranean stream. You become aware of them in your dreams and in quiet times of prayer

4 "Reminiscences of Julia Ward Howe," *Atlantic Monthly* 83 (1889): 707.

and contemplation. In the liminal time between sleeping and waking, when the maintenance hole cover is off, you're bold to descend the ladder and board a rubber raft, riding the wild current until you see light beams illuminating another ladder, leading upward. Climbing it back into consciousness, you safely make your exit.

Over the course of many brief excursions, it's possible to sketch out a rough map, indicating where entry and exit points may be found. Your illuminations database—along with any spiritual journal you may happen to keep—forms a significant portion of this map. Works of visual art, music, and poetry may likewise point the way to these access points, so it's important to make time in your life for these.

Make no mistake, nothing you write could ever provide a comprehensive plan of the aqueduct system beneath your feet. But you don't need to map it. You just need to know where some good access points may be found. Because God is the architect of this aqueduct system, you can trust the flow of the dark river to bear you along, even if none of us know in fullest detail where it's going.

One of the greatest services you provide your people, as a preacher, is to find those access points, note their location, and return to them whenever you need to show others the wild beauty that may be found there. They can drop their buckets, then, for a drink, but the boldest among them will choose to do more. They will make their own journeys to the dark river, cheered on by you as their guide.

One of the most ancient titles for ministers is a steward of the mysteries of God. By no means can you or anyone claim full mastery of dreams and visions, but in this humble river-keeper function, you acknowledge you know just enough to curate them. This is what it means to be a steward of the mysteries. Our people look to us to do this.

Some people—myself included, at times—mystically attribute wee-hours revelations to the Holy Spirit. That may well be true, but there's a more prosaic explanation for those who need one. Sleep medicine researchers suggest that dreams are the brain's way of intuitively solving certain problems. Whether you attribute such insights to divine intervention, to the brain's nightly cognitive retooling, or to both, the important thing about this method is that *it works*.

Norman Maclean, son of a Presbyterian minister, turns to the spiritual symbolism of flowing water in his semi-autobiographical novel, *A River Runs Through It*. The book concludes with a well-known paean to fly-fishing among the rocks and boulders of a swift-flowing Montana river—a skill his father taught him in his youth. Of course, it's about much more than that:

> Now nearly all those I loved and did not understand when I was young are dead, but I still reach out to them.
>
> Of course, now I am too old to be much of a fisherman, and now of course I usually fish the big waters alone, although some friends think I shouldn't. Like many fly fishermen in western Montana where the summer days are almost Arctic in length, I often do not start fishing until the cool of the evening. Then in the Arctic half-light of the canyon, all existence fades to a being with my soul and memories and the sounds of the Big Blackfoot River and a four-count rhythm and the hope that a fish will rise.
>
> Eventually, all things merge into one, and a river runs through it. The river was cut by the world's great flood and runs over rocks from the beginning of time. On some of the rocks are timeless raindrops. Under the rocks are the words, and some of the words are theirs.
>
> I am haunted by waters.[5]

REIGNITING THE SHIMMER

Dream insights, of course—fascinating and wondrous as they are—can't be summoned on demand. You can hedge your bets by

5 Norman Maclean, *A River Runs Through It* (University of Chicago Press, 1989), 161.

consulting your database. It's through the process of retrieval that a homiletical database yields up its secrets.

Rowling's Harry Potter novels tell of a high-security section within the Ministry of Magic's headquarters known as the Department of Mysteries. The wizards who work in that unit study mysteries like love, space, thought, time, and death. One dark room within the Department of Mysteries is the Hall of Prophecy:

> They were there, they had found the place: high as a church and full of nothing but towering shelves covered in small, dusty, glass orbs. They glimmered dully in the light issuing from more candle brackets set at intervals along the shelves. Like those in the circular room behind them, their flames were burning blue.[6]

Each glass orb contains a record of a prophecy, labeled with the name of the wizard who discerned it, along with the person whom the prophecy concerns and the year it was made. Some orbs contain a milky white liquid, warm to the touch and softly glowing with an inner light. Others remain "dull and dark as blown light bulbs."[7]

What Rowling is describing is a walk-in database. Some of the archived prophecies are live, meaning they have yet to be fulfilled. Others have expired, either because they've been fulfilled or because they've been magically blocked in some way. The live ones are the ones that shimmer.

Sermon illuminations are not prophecies, of course, but the ones we later treasure do retain something of their original shimmer—the glow we first noticed about them. Even so, the quarry may elude us. The theological concepts we struggle to teach are highly abstract. As we've seen in chapter 1, the artifacts that shimmer are those that help us render highly abstract concepts into concrete form.

---

6 J. K. Rowling, *Harry Potter and the Order of the Phoenix* (Scholastic, 2003), 777.

7 Rowling, *Harry Potter and the Order of the Phoenix*, 777.

CHAPTER FOUR

The Collaborator

Borrowing with Integrity

In the world of museums, it's well established that you can't put on a world-class special exhibition without doing some borrowing. Curators of the first rank are expected to be familiar not only with the contents of their own museum's warehouse but also with the holdings of similar culture palaces around the world. Touring a museum's permanent galleries, you may come across a blank space on the wall or an empty pedestal on which a little card has been hung—sometimes accompanied with a photograph—announcing that the artwork usually displayed there is on loan to another museum.

On the other side of the exchange, as you attend a special exhibition, you may see a corresponding card thanking the lending institution for making the loaned item available. "Share and share alike" is a guiding principle of the museum world.

No doubt, a certain amount of horse-trading goes on behind the scenes. Maybe a loaned item is offered in exchange for another. Or maybe some money changes hands. In some cases, artifacts may be loaned simply for the good of the museum-going public—accompanied by a vaguely expressed hope that, should an occasion arise for returning the favor, the recipient will look kindly on such a request.

No one faults special-exhibition curators for looking beyond their own museum's collection for the best artworks to display. More often, they're praised for their knowledge of the field and for their negotiating chops. Likewise, as you curate your sermon illuminations, you also take up the task of a collaborator, recognizing that you do need to collaborate with colleagues from time to time, borrowing material from them.

Borrowing illuminations for sermons is a whole lot simpler than borrowing artifacts from museums. Preachers work with blocks of text, not one-of-a-kind creations painted on canvas or sculpted from marble. To borrow from another writer's work leaves no empty space on the gallery wall. It requires no permission, other than the fair-use provisions of copyright law, and such law applies only if the sermon manuscript is eventually published. Rarely are authors even aware that, somewhere on a Sunday morning, a preacher has echoed a line or two from one of their published works.

Congregations typically praise preachers who are well read and skilled at augmenting their own message with wise words of others. Problems arise only if the borrowing preacher makes a fundamental mistake: failing to mention that the item is borrowed. Most congregations assume that the language you use in the pulpit is your own unless you notify them otherwise. If they discover you've been systematically passing off the words of others as your own, without attribution, the consequences could be swift, negative, and severe—possibly even end-of-your-ministry severe.

It's really that simple. There's no need to clutter a sermon manuscript with the detailed sort of footnotes common in academic papers. It's enough to say "The preacher Fred Craddock once told this story" or even to offer the generic attribution "The story is told . . ." This last example is especially useful for those timeless, anonymous jokes and anecdotes that make the rounds.

To do otherwise is plagiarism—a word you've no doubt encountered many times in the course of your education. Plagiarism is especially frowned upon in academic circles, and it's no less odious in the pulpit. It should be even more problematic for preaching because of our fundamental purpose, which is to lead our listeners to know God better.

The English word *plagiarism* has its origin in the Greek *plagion* and the Latin *plagium*, both of which mean "kidnapping." Is there any congregation, anywhere, who wants a kidnapper for a pastor?

YOU CAN'T FAKE AUTHENTICITY

Numerous studies of effective ministry have been conducted over the years, generating lists of talents to be identified and skills to be mastered. Along with all the skill-based categories you'd expect, there's one pastoral attribute that tops nearly all these lists: authenticity.

Our principal task as pastors, particularly as preachers, is to tell the truth. We're bearers of the good news of Jesus Christ. If we show ourselves to be unfaithful in the telling of it, few listeners will allow us into their hearts again.

The writer Barry Lopez tells of a conversation he once had with a traditional American Indian storyteller. It taught him something, he said, about how to distinguish authentic stories from inauthentic ones. The anonymous storyteller told him: "An authentic story is about us, an inauthentic story is about you."[1]

It's a key distinction to recall in choosing stories for the pulpit. Anyone can tell a secondhand story, but it's more authentic to retell the same story from your own perspective. This is not stealing the story—telling it as though it happened to you—but rather telling how you received it. Authenticizing a secondhand story can be as simple as beginning your retelling like this: "Here's a story that, when I heard it, made me think about my faith more deeply." Such a move transforms the story into a metastory. It focuses on how the original

1 Cited by Mark Yaconelli, *Between the Listening and the Telling: How Stories Can Save Us* (Broadleaf Books, 2022), 78.

story impacted you, which then invites the listener to receive it in a similar way as you honestly retell it.

To put it simply, there's nothing wrong with using canned sermon material as long as you're the one doing the canning. Just don't pretend you grew the string beans.

Let us never lose track of preaching's testimonial character. A sermon is not an exegesis lecture, a news commentary, or a call to social activism, although it may include elements of all these things. At its very heart, a sermon testifies to your experiences with God in a way that frees others to seek out their own unique experiences.

Beware of the temptation to preach what some call a teaching sermon. This is often a thinly veiled lecture, in many cases explaining liturgical or sacramental practices or some fine point of exegesis or psychology. In no sense is a sermon the same as a lecture. Such a message may contain true and even valuable information, but if it's lacking in testimonial character, it simply isn't a sermon. Informing the mind is a worthy task, but that's the work of professors. Moving the heart is the vocation of pastors.

I can recall two particular experiences of disillusionment regarding a preacher's attempt to fake authenticity through pulpit plagiarism. Both came from my perspective in the pew, not the pulpit.

The first of these experiences took place during my seminary years. I was doing field education in a congregation served by an interim pastor. He was a recently retired preacher of some renown in the local area who'd agreed to fill the pulpit. He'd also agreed to supervise two weekend seminary interns, one of whom was me.

My field education partner and I were just getting to know him. We hadn't chosen each other as supervisor and learners, but the sudden departure of the previous pastor had thrown us together, and we were determined to make the best of it.

On one of his first Sundays in the pulpit, I read his sermon title in the printed bulletin: "The Importance of Doubting Your Doubts."

"What a great title!" I said to myself. But something about it sounded naggingly familiar.

His sermon was outstanding in every way, particularly in its delivery. This man had an old-fashioned "prince of the pulpit" oratorical style—a much-admired trait back then. The congregation loved it. But that uneasy sense of familiarity lingered.

Back in my dorm room on the seminary campus, I pulled one of my recently purchased textbooks off the shelf. It was an anthology of great historical sermons for my introductory preaching course. There in the table of contents I saw it: "The Importance of Doubting Your Doubts" by Harry Emerson Fosdick, the renowned pastor of New York City's Riverside Church in the early twentieth century.

Reading through Fosdick's original sermon, I realized that my new supervisor hadn't plagiarized the entire thing, but he had swiped roughly a third of it, along with the intriguing title. That portion of his sermon had been word-for-word identical to Fosdick's. He offered no attribution to the original author. So far as the congregation knew, every word had been his own original work.

I walked across the hall to the room where my field education partner lived. I showed him the sermon anthology. The two of us knew, then, what topic we would suggest for the next Sunday's supervisory session.

Back at the church the next Sunday afternoon, I shared with our supervisor what I'd discovered. He flushed. He hemmed and hawed. Then he said something about how, once the two of us were out of seminary, we'd learn how all preachers borrow liberally from one another. It was all right, he said. Common practice. It was even a good thing to know the best published sermon material out there and powerfully present it.

He was right. I did learn something that day. I learned that here was a man who could not be trusted.

The second plagiarism experience is of more recent vintage. It involves a single story told from the pulpit. But that's all it takes to puncture the balloon of pastoral authenticity forever.

At this point in my ministry, I had a couple of decades of preaching experience behind me. A new congregation of our denomination was being chartered at a special Sunday afternoon service. I was present as one of a team of ministers leading the celebration.

The preacher that day—a recently arrived pastor at a notable tall-steeple church in our area—did a splendid job. His sermon included a little story of an incident that, he told us, had recently happened in his church's nursery school. He said one of the teachers had shared it with him.

There was a little boy in that class who had only one arm. The class was learning the old finger game that goes like this: "Here is the church and here is the steeple. Open the doors, and see all the people!"

The teacher said, "OK, class, now turn to the boy or girl next to you and show your partner how you make a church."

As soon as the words fell from her mouth, she recalled with horror the boy with one arm. She was afraid he'd feel embarrassed. She'd unwittingly drawn attention to his disability.

But it turned out just fine. The little girl next to him smiled and said brightly, "Give me your hand. Let's make a church together!"

It was a perfect—if overly cute—addition to his sermon on that occasion of making a new church. But my inner reaction to his homey little story was that, once again, it sounded oddly familiar.

Back home, I sat down at my computer—a resource unavailable in my earlier, pre-internet seminary days—and googled a few keywords. I saw not one but dozens of versions of the same story, all of them in sermons by other preachers. Some of them dated back ten years or more, longer than this preacher had been in his present congregation.

Clearly, he'd deployed one of those old chestnuts. But here's the problem. He didn't present it by saying "The story is told . . ." or "Have you ever heard the story about . . .?" He distinctly told us the incident took place in his church's nursery school.

Maybe it had. Maybe, through some unlikely coincidence, it just happened to be identical to the timeworn pulpit tale. But I doubt it. More likely, he figured the story would have a bigger impact if he gave it a local habitation and a name in his own church.

Maybe I should have followed the advice of Matthew 15:15 by making an appointment with my pastoral colleague to "point out the fault when the two of you are alone." But I didn't. I had no appetite for such confrontation. My inner response, though, was the same as it had been in the case of my former field education supervisor. Could I trust this colleague who had been unfaithful in small things to be faithful in bigger things?

Both these tales I've just told come from an earlier time. The first happened before the internet, and the second in the early days of Google searches. Since then, we preachers have become ever more dependent on the cloud, which is a great blessing.

But it can also be a curse. Yes, there's a universe of inspiring and informative sermon resources out there, ready to be cut and pasted. Today's web browsers make that act of cutting and pasting almost too easy. You can slip into plagiarism before you know it. My old field education supervisor was a lot more intentional. He sat at his typewriter with a book of Fosdick's sermons open in front of him. Letter by letter, he pecked out the text he was stealing. With today's technology, any of us could commit the same heist in seconds.

But here's something else that's changed. The same thing can now happen in reverse. The sermon manuscripts you post on your church website or in your personal blog are just as susceptible to discovery and harvesting by others. More than a few preachers—including, sadly, some I number among my friends—have faced disciplinary charges because an antagonist in their congregation ran their sermons through antiplagiarism software of the sort used by university professors. A determined antagonist doesn't even need specialized software to do this. Cutting and pasting a few lines into the Google search box can be just as incriminating. I've seen otherwise effective ministries go down in flames for want of a few words of source attribution.

Chicken thieves of old, fresh from slaughtering their prey, were famously caught red-handed by the sheriff. Today's careless preachers can be caught red-handed because of how they thoughtlessly use their computer keyboards.

So does this mean you can never use the words of others in your sermons? Of course not. You should do so fearlessly and often. It's not a question of whether you can use borrowed material but how.

At the heart of that how is remaining conscious that what you're communicating is your own joy of discovery. All preaching is, at the root, come-and-see testimony. In the famous words of Bishop D. T. Niles of the Church of South India, in matters of evangelism we're one beggar telling another beggar where to get food. To throw in a quick source reference (as I've just done in the previous sentence) requires very little effort and in no way weakens your testimony. Quite the contrary: Such casual honesty communicates how determined you are to practice scholarly humility. The last time I checked, humility is still a Christian virtue.

You may imagine the story you're retelling as a gleaming piece of beach glass, but in reality it's not the glass but the shimmer—your experience of it—you're sharing. You're speaking not as the authority who created it, or as a diligent researcher who ferreted it out of some obscure text, but as a fellow pilgrim who happened to run across it and delight in it. Share your joy! Remember that basic principle and it's unlikely you'll ever stumble into plagiarism.

INVASION OF THE AVATARS

On June 9, 2023, a congregation of three hundred or so gathered in a Protestant church in the Bavarian town of Fürth for a worship service likely to be remembered as historic. For the first time in human history, a congregation of God's people participated in a worship service entirely conceived and presented by computers using generative AI. The experimental service took place as part of the *Kirchentag*, the biennial gathering of mostly Protestant Christians from across Germany and the world.[2]

---

2 Kirsten Grieshaber, "Can a Chatbot Preach a Good Sermon? Hundreds Attend Church Service Generated by ChatGPT to Find Out,"

During the Covid-19 pandemic, people of faith across the globe grew familiar—if not entirely comfortable—with worship services conducted online using electronic conferencing technology. Even prior to the pandemic, members of certain megachurches had grown well used to similar technological whizbangery as senior leaders beamed their services from the mothership to satellite congregations. Some such services are presented synchronously (in real time) and others asynchronously (recently recorded).

In these examples, everyone sitting at their computers knows that, if they could somehow ride the stream of electrons back to their source, they would find living, breathing human beings standing before the cameras, either at that very moment or in the recent past. Not so with the worship service in Fürth. The four figures leading worship on the central screen—two young men and two young women—were avatars: computer-generated images, speaking and gesturing exactly as the AI-enabled computer had created them to do. A professor at the University of Vienna, a theologian and philosopher named Jonas Simmerlein had keyed in the instructions the computers used to animate them, so the worship service was not completely lacking in human input. "I conceived this service—but actually I rather accompanied it, because I would say about ninety-eight percent comes from the machine," explained Simmerlein. "I told the artificial intelligence 'We are at the church congress, you are a preacher—what would a church service look like?'"[3] Simmerlein also asked the computer to include psalms, as well as prayers and a closing benediction. Clearly, the avatars offered no handshakes at the church door.

If Simmerlein's estimate of 2 percent input from him was correct, it was important input indeed. He instructed the computer to base the service on the *Kirchentag*'s 2023 theme, "Now is the time." The resulting sermon mentioned topics such as leaving the past behind,

---

Associated Press, June 10, 2023, https://apnews.com/article/germany-church-protestants-chatgpt-ai-sermon-651f21c24cfb47e3122e987a7263d348.

3 Grieshaber, "Can a Chatbot Preach a Good Sermon?"

never losing faith, and ironically—considering who was speaking—overcoming the fear of death.

The congregation's response, by all accounts, was mixed. Sometimes the avatars' deadpan presentation evoked laughter, and so did a banal platitude one of them uttered: "To keep our faith, we must pray and go to church regularly." Such rough edges can be attributed to the newness of AI technology, which is still in its infancy. It's not hard to imagine that, in days to come, AI-enabled preaching avatars will appear, from a purely technical standpoint, to be indistinguishable from the real thing.

But will they?

It's perilous to peer into the future and try to answer that question this early in the avatar dynasty, but my initial response is "Relax, go about your business, there's nothing to see here." Maybe it could be an issue for megachurch pastors, whose people primarily know them as talking heads on a screen, but not for pastors of smaller congregations, whose ministry is more high touch than high tech. Phillips Brooks's classic definition of preaching as "the bringing of truth through personality" still holds.[4] Christian testimony is a good deal more than an aggregation of words. Significantly, it's a meeting of hearts—and a computer's central processing unit will never be able to carry off such a feat.

Prognostication becomes murkier regarding AI assistance with generating material for illuminating sermons. It's possible, even now, to instruct an AI engine to write five sermon illustrations on kindness. Seconds later, the machine will produce five paragraph-long anecdotes demonstrating human kindness, complete with fictional names for the characters. Such stories are bland and utterly generic: No spark of human personality evident there.

Altering the instruction slightly by asking the computer to search the internet for five sermon illustrations on kindness, the AI program spits out five generic stories or metaphors related to kindness. (When

---

4 Phillips Brooks, *Lectures on Preaching: Delivered Before the Divinity School of Yale College in January and February, 1877* (Macmillan, 1907), 5.

I tried this, one of the stories was a summary version of Jesus's parable of the good Samaritan.)

Google and other search engine providers are hard at work integrating AI language-learning capabilities into their programs, generating increasingly accurate results. No matter how useful the output may appear to be, though, it's still vital to dig deeper than the search engine results themselves, verifying the original sources the AI program claims to have located. In these early days of AI-enhanced search, there have been alarming examples of fabricated results that sound plausible but in fact have no relation to reality.

Writing in *The New York Times*, linguistics professors Noam Chomsky and Ian Roberts, along with AI expert Jeffrey Watumull, collaborated on a moral examination of the strengths and weaknesses of ChatGPT, one of the best-known AI applications. Their conclusion follows:

> ChatGPT exhibits something like the banality of evil: plagiarism and apathy and obviation. It summarizes the standard arguments in the literature by a kind of super-autocomplete, refuses to take a stand on anything, pleads not merely ignorance but lack of intelligence and ultimately offers a "just following orders" defense, shifting responsibility to its creators.
>
> In short, ChatGPT and its brethren are constitutionally unable to balance creativity with constraint. They either overgenerate (producing both truths and falsehoods, endorsing ethical and unethical decisions alike) or undergenerate (exhibiting noncommitment to any decisions and indifference to consequences). Given the amorality, faux science and linguistic incompetence of these systems, we can only laugh or cry at their popularity.[5]

---

5 Noam Chomsky et al., "Noam Chomsky: The False Promise of ChatGPT," *New York Times*, March 8, 2023, https://www.nytimes.com/2023/03/08/opinion/noam-chomsky-chatgpt-ai.html.

That may have been so in 2023, but stay tuned. AI technology is changing rapidly.

It's been possible for some time to use search engines to find lists of sermon illustrations on various topics, but those results simply point to web pages previously created by human beings. It won't be long before AI-equipped search engines will be able to skip the middle step of a human author or editor and will themselves be able to comb through millions of online sermon manuscripts in the blink of an eye, presenting the most frequently chosen examples of stories that illuminate the requested topic.

When that day arrives, the question to ask about AI-enabled search—or even next-generation avatar preachers—will be whether they display any capability to seek, recognize, and communicate the shimmer of discovery that's so essential to sparking inspiration. Color me unconvinced that such a feat will ever be possible.

CHAPTER FIVE

The Designer

Imagining the Sequence

In my early years of preaching, I carefully outlined each message. But I soon learned that my sermons that elicited the strongest response were those I'd planned in a different way. I started taking risks. I jumped into designing my sermons without a preplanned outline, looking to the illuminations selected by the reference librarian in me to arrange themselves in a coherent and engaging way. I never neglected the Scripture text, but I no longer felt I had to begin with it.

Sometimes it worked better to start by telling a story that engaged the imagination and then sidling up to the Scripture. Other times—especially if something had happened in the news or in the congregation's life that was on everyone's mind—it worked better to explore the dimensions of a human problem, turning to the Scriptures only later in search of solutions. I never knew for sure which way I would go until I'd had the chance to lay out the various illumination materials I had retrieved and explore how they fit together.

In museum curation, this is the work of a special-exhibition designer whose task is to select, out of an aggregation of likely prospects, the best of the best pieces to display. As a preacher, your design phase is when you sort through your retrieved illuminations that are most closely related to your text and topic and decide on the order in which you'll present them. Ideally, the result will have a cognitive dimension but also deal mightily in emotion. The best sermons have a logical argument at their heart, but they draw listeners through the argument by touching hearts as well as minds.

This design process is not so random as it may appear. In your exegetical study of the text, you've identified one or more theological topic words. Months—even years—before, you've filed away illumination material under those same topic words. You didn't know it at the time, but you were actually doing advance work on a sermon you didn't know you'd be preaching. Searching your database using the same topic words, you've just pulled out a handful of found objects that seem to you to shimmer still. There's a common theological thread running through them all: You simply need to experiment with different arrangements of those beads along the string until the right pattern emerges.

There's a trial-and-error process to it, like doing a jigsaw puzzle. You start with the straight-edge pieces and progress from there, using the contours of each piece to choose the next one. By the time you get to the closing prayer, a coherent picture has emerged.

I like to think about it as building a fieldstone wall.

ONE MORE STONE IN THE WALL

When pioneering farmers first introduced iron plowshares to rocky New England soil, they swiftly realized what a difficult task they'd undertaken. Unlike the soft black soil of European farms, cultivated for centuries, these new farmsteads were studded with glacial rocks. Plowing a field was tough going. Farmers repeatedly had to pry stones out of the soil and carry them off to the edges of their newly cleared fields. They would repeat this action over many growing seasons as their plowshare kept turning up fresh obstacles.

Fortunately, there was a ready use for these stonepiles. The stones could be repurposed to create low walls, separating one field from another. You can see these fieldstone walls all over New England to this day, even in places where marginal farms have long since been abandoned and wild forest has reclaimed the land.

Fieldstone walls are more than haphazard piles of rocks. Building them is a complex and intricate craft—selecting and positioning just the right stones to take their proper place in the wall, all without mortar. Wall builders depend on sophisticated spatial reasoning to envision the gaps that need to be filled, then they match that negative space with the stones they have on hand. Occasionally they split a few with a hammer and chisel. But mostly, they rely on their own eyes as they choose just the right one. If they do their work well, the wall they construct will last for centuries, through many a winter freeze and spring thaw.

The items you pile up in your homiletical staging area are like those random heaps of stones. Placement requires considerable precision. Stoneworkers rely on a string stretched tight between temporary wooden posts—not an outline but a guideline—ensuring that the wall remains straight. They hang another string from the top of their latest section of wall, and from it they dangle a small piece of lead known as a plumb bob (*plumbum* in Latin means "lead"). One of the most ancient construction tools, the plumb bob unfailingly displays the influence of gravity. The plumb-bob string defines the wall's vertical dimension, just as the taut ground-level string guides the horizontal. If the new section is out of plumb, it needs to be torn down and replaced with a different configuration of stones or else the structure will not endure for long.

Lest your sermons become a haphazard succession of one disconnected anecdote after another, you need taut strings to guide you. A detailed outline can accomplish this, of course, but in many cases that's overkill. Those farmer-stonemasons didn't need architectural blueprints, after all. You do need to know, generally, where the argument is headed—intuiting what God may be saying through the Scripture as well as what outcome to expect from your listeners. Your topic sentence is an important guideline in this regard. You also need to know, as you lay one stone atop another, whether your efforts remain in plumb with the theological principles your exegesis has revealed.

Within those guidelines, your rummaging through the stonepile becomes a matter of intuition as you ponder the negative spaces. You keep in mind not only the stones already placed but also others you've pulled from the pile as likely candidates.

The spaces between the stones are the transitions between items. Transitions aren't easily worked out in advance because each one is formed by the shape of the stones that surround it. Just as spaces in a wall link individual stones, listeners need such gaps to discern the larger shape that's emerging.

We've been envisioning the fieldstone wall as a single sermon. But you can also imagine it symbolizing a larger, ongoing project: your entire preaching ministry to that congregation. Scripture texts and sermon topics naturally vary, but viewed in the larger sense of proclaiming the gospel, you're returning to the same wall each Lord's Day to add a new section. You build on what's gone before, looking ahead to sections yet to come. As long as you attend to the diversity of Scripture texts—either by following a lectionary or pursuing a preaching plan of your own devising—you can reasonably expect, in time, to share the totality of the gospel.

With respect to those stones you've yanked from the field that now reside in the stonepile, they are of four principal types: metaphors, stories, poetry, and quotations. We'll consider each of these principal categories in turn. But first, here are some practical hints about organizing the illumination material you've pulled from your database.

ENVISIONING THROUGH A STORYBOARD

The simplest way to manage your staging area is to cut and paste the brief snippets of text, in random order, into a blank word-processing document. As you do so, you can highlight either the title you gave it in your database or some other identifying phrase. A little later, as you scroll through this data dump of randomly ordered material, the highlights remind you of what each block of text is about. Think of the highlighted bits as the tabs on old-fashioned manila folders.

If you have an unusually large number of items to sequence, an alternative method can be to prepare a rough table of contents, using that feature in your word-processing program. The order in which items appear is irrelevant at this point: This is not an actual table of contents for your sermon but rather a quick index of the collection of material you've assembled for possible use. That table of contents will never see the light of day beyond your study. It's a temporary organizing tool giving you a rough overview of the illuminations you've pulled out for consideration.

Think of these strategies as a form of storyboarding.

The word *storyboarding* comes from the film industry. At a certain stage of movie production, a number of scenes have already been filmed or at least sketched out in the script. Now the time has come to sequence them, envisioning which ones will ultimately appear in the theatrical version and in what order. The movie's script—similar to a sermon outline—provides significant guidance, but the script is always provisional.

Walt Disney and his animators used storyboarding extensively as they developed classic full-length feature cartoons like *Snow White and the Seven Dwarfs* and *Dumbo*. Because preparing animation cels in that precomputer era was so labor-intensive (the artists painted individual images dozens, even hundreds, of times before they were filmed), the movie's director needed to try out various dramatic sequences before committing the studio's animators to weeks of pointless toil. For them to complete those scenes only to be told their work lacked something vital and would have to be discarded was demoralizing in the extreme—not to mention a waste of the company's human and financial resources.

What was needed was a way to try out the possibilities ahead of time. Disney commissioned some of his best animators to roughly sketch images in pencil, using not costly animation cels but plain paper. They thumbtacked the papers to a bulletin board. The director could then move the images around, experimenting with various scenarios. Everyone knew these sketches were not the final product but merely a step along the way. It was important for everyone to step away from the grind of applying paint to celluloid to get a bird's-eye view of the project. At this stage, they needed to see the forest, not the trees.

The same is true for designing a sermon. Sometimes the natural arc of a biblical story dictates the order of scenes. Often, it's best to retell the story just as the biblical writer gives it to you. But not always. Just as Hollywood movies sometimes make use of flashbacks and other narrative devices, there are other ways to bring the narrative to life in a fresh-sounding way.

Sometimes—particularly when you're preaching on the letters of Paul and other apostles—the text is making a complex theological argument, addressing a specific problem convulsing one of the New Testament churches. To import every detail of such an argument into the life of a modern congregation, whose own challenges are different, is to board a fast train to irrelevance. Better to recast the argument into terms today's listeners can easily apply to their own lives.

Other times, especially with more topical sermons, there's greater freedom to experiment with various logical sequences. Many sermon topics cry out for a reasoned argument, a logical progression from one point to the next. This could be a simple list of action steps—a plan familiar to consumers of self-help articles or online TED Talks (e.g., "Five Steps to Overcoming Insecurity"). Or it could reflect a more nuanced argument (if not this, not this, and not this, then *that*). It could take a descent-ascent form: first highlighting a common problem and then accompanying the listeners on a downward path of growing anxiety before presenting a solution and guiding them upward again, touting the benefits of that course of action.

Much more could be said about constructing logical arguments, but our chief concern here is not the overall sermon design but the role illuminations play within that design. Certain illuminations naturally fall into one stage of the argument or another. Others are more adaptable, fitting in almost anywhere. The sequencing, or storyboarding, phase is made for experimentation.

Sometimes, particularly with narrative material, the illumination may be substantial enough to serve as an entire point of the sermon. This technique can certainly be overused—we've all listened to sermons that are little more than random assortments of anecdotes—but matched to the right text, it can be very powerful. We've already noted Craddock's genius in simply telling a homespun tale and leaving it to the listeners to connect the dots. In such a case, transitions take on major importance, indicating how the story relates to the overall argument as well as to the material before and after.

One advantage of the storyboarding process is that it helps you quickly see which sorts of material you have in abundance and which are lacking. If two illuminations or quotations appear repetitive, it's an easy matter at this stage to jettison one of the storyboard panels, saving it for another occasion. Storyboarding may also reveal a gap crying out to be filled, prompting a further, focused search.

Storyboards are an alternative form of sermon outline. Their chief advantage is that they're more malleable and adaptable. I've already mentioned a few principal categories of illuminations whose basic forms may appear on the storyboard panels. These are metaphors, stories, poetry, and quotations.

Metaphors: Talking in Pictures

We all know what metaphors are. In his *Poetics*, Aristotle praises them, saying, "The greatest thing by far is to be a master of metaphor. It is the one thing that cannot be learnt from others; and it is also a sign of genius, since a good metaphor implies an intuitive perception of the similarity in dissimilars."[1]

Describing exactly how metaphors work, though, is surprisingly difficult. Shakespeare takes a stab at capturing their function in these famous lines from act 5, scene 1 of *A Midsummer Night's Dream*:

---

1 Aristotle, *Poetics*, trans. Gerald F. Else (University of Michigan Press, 1967), 1459a 5–8.

The poet's eye, in a fine frenzy rolling,
Doth glance from heaven to Earth, from Earth to heaven;
And as imagination bodies forth
The forms of things unknown, the poet's pen
Turns them to shapes, and gives to airy nothing
A local habitation and a name.
Such tricks hath strong imagination,
That if it would but apprehend some joy,
It comprehends some bringer of that joy;
Or in the night, imagining some fear,
How easy is a bush supposed a bear!

Metaphor "bodies forth the forms of things unknown." Notice that the vehicle by which these airy forms take shape is imagination. Think about that word: how prominent the word *image* is within it. Metaphor makers craft images. They think in pictures. Each image carries a world of meaning, requiring "a fine frenzy" of words to conjure it into existence. In tending toward the concrete rather than the abstract, metaphor clothes abstract concepts with "a local habitation and a name."

We carelessly think we understand the meaning of *joy*—which is, after all, a very common English word. Yet no dictionary definition communicates that word's deep meaning like the image of a bright-eyed, grinning child sitting under a Christmas tree, opening a long-anticipated gift. The dictionary is correct in defining joy as a feeling of great pleasure and happiness, but only the ancient alchemy of metaphor transports us beyond the bare dictionary definition to "comprehend some bringer of that joy."

Metaphors function like the outrigger on a Polynesian canoe. Those renowned mariners could sail away from their coral atoll homes only because they'd discovered how to double their canoes' stability by adding an outrigger. Similarly, deploying a metaphor in a sermon is more than mere aesthetic decoration. It strengthens and stabilizes your argument, making it both more understandable and more memorable.

C. S. Lewis celebrates the unique power of metaphors to convey meaning in an obscure essay, "Bluspels and Flalansferes: A Semantic Nightmare." In it, he derides certain modern philosophers who denigrate metaphor as imprecise—favoring abstract scientific language instead—calling them "among the least significant of writers."[2] Not so for imaginative thinkers who freely make use of metaphor:

> But open your Plato, and you will find yourself among the great creators of metaphor, and therefore among the masters of meaning. If we turn to Theology—or rather to the literature of religion—the result will be more surprising still; for unless our whole argument is wrong, we shall have to admit that a man who says heaven and thinks of the visible sky is pretty sure to mean more than a man who tells us that heaven is a state of mind. . . . But it must not be supposed that I am in any sense putting forward the imagination as the organ of truth. We are not talking of truth, but of meaning: meaning which is the antecedent condition both of truth and falsehood, whose antithesis is not error but nonsense. I am a rationalist. For me, reason is the natural organ of truth; but imagination is the organ of meaning. Imagination, producing new metaphors or revivifying old, is not the cause of truth, but its condition. It is, I confess, undeniable that such a view indirectly implies a kind of truth or rightness in the imagination itself.[3]

Let's consider for a moment this example Lewis uses: the sky as a metaphor for heaven. I can recall several of my seminary professors in the late 1970s declaring it was time to cease using such imagery in liturgy. Our congregants had recent memories of watching the grainy black-and-white TV images of astronauts Neil Armstrong and Buzz Aldrin walking on the moon. They'd heard how Soviet Premier

---

2 C. S. Lewis, "Bluspels and Flalansferes: A Semantic Nightmare," *Rehabilitations and Other Essays* (Oxford University Press, 1939), 133.

3 Lewis, "Bluspels and Flalansferes," 133.

Nikita Khrushchev—referencing cosmonaut Yuri Gagarin, the first human in space—had ridiculed religion, saying, "Gagarin flew into space, but didn't see any god there." Heavenly sky metaphors, those seminary professors concluded, were outmoded and anti-scientific. A space-age church had no business lifting up praises to the Almighty because everyone knew perfectly well God isn't up there. (I'm not sure those theologians had thought through how to interpret the biblical accounts of Jesus's ascension, but no doubt they were working on it.)

I believe—and Lewis would surely agree—those professors displayed an impoverished understanding of metaphor. The most important question is: Which language choice conveys, most simply and elegantly, not the truth of heaven but its meaning, the classic biblical imagery of God riding upon the clouds or calling heaven a state of mind or the focus of our ultimate concern? More to the point, which of these will preach?

Bundles of Meaning

Brain scientists, using fMRI scans to study complex thought patterns, have noticed that entire clusters of neurons light up when the brain is processing higher-level material. This neural bottleneck naturally limits the amount of material the brain can handle at any one moment. But if a previous memory is recalled, a much smaller area lights up. The brain can handle this material more easily because it's already bundled it—saving not each discrete memory but the larger pattern. The bundle is now a single unit rather than a cluster of individual experiences. It requires less cognitive processing power.

We do something similar every day as we recall ten-digit phone numbers. We're quite used to mentally storing these numbers in a 3–3–4 pattern (area code, exchange, and number). We can handle that bundled data more easily than trying to recall a string of ten digits. In the same way, when counting out a great number of items using pencil and paper, we make use of tally marks—those bundles of four vertical lines tied together by a diagonal line. When the last item has been counted, it's easy to tote up the number of bundles and multiply by five. In a more physical example, the ancient craft of thatching a roof requires the thatcher to first bundle together many stalks of dried grass and then transport the bundles to the roof and tie them together. Flinging the equivalent amount of loose hay onto the roof with a pitchfork would lead to misery during the next rainstorm. There's magic in the bundling.

But metaphor hunting is more than just a physiological process. Yes, metaphors do bundle meaning. They allow the brain to reuse previously constructed pathways. But they do so using imaginative images that are notoriously difficult to analyze. What is it that makes one metaphorical image work and another fail? That seems more a matter of art than science.

In *Harry Potter and the Prisoner of Azkaban*, the budding young wizards at Hogwarts School take classes in the care of magical creatures. One of the weird beasts the gamekeeper Hagrid introduces to Harry and his friends is a highly intelligent animal known as a hippogriff:

> Trotting towards them were a dozen of the most bizarre creatures Harry had ever seen. They had the bodies, hind legs and tails of horses, but the front legs, wings and heads of what seemed to be giant eagles, with cruel, steel-coloured beaks and large, brilliantly orange eyes. The talons on their front legs were half a foot long and deadly-looking. Each of the beasts had a thick leather collar around its neck, which was attached to a long chain, and the ends of all of these were held in the vast hands of Hagrid, who came jogging into the paddock behind the creatures.[4]

Hippogriffs will allow you to ride them through the air, Hagrid explains, but they're not yours to command. You must treat a

---

4 J. K. Rowling, *Harry Potter and the Prisoner of Azkaban* (Scholastic, 1999), 113–14.

hippogriff with unfailing tact and diplomacy. It's not so much that you choose the beast you'll ride; your hippogriff also chooses you. Before you try to mount one, there's a certain protocol you must carefully follow:

> "Yeh always wait fer the Hippogriff ter make the firs' move," Hagrid continued. "It's polite, see? Yeh walk towards him, and yeh bow, an' yeh wait. If he bows back, yeh're allowed ter touch him. If he doesn' bow, then get away from him sharpish, 'cause those talons hurt."[5]

Just as there's a certain amount of trial and error in choosing a hippogriff, the same is true of choosing metaphors for abstract ideas to ride. Some metaphors are apt. Others are disastrous mismatches. It's not easy to say why one metaphor works and another doesn't. It's almost as though they're sentient creatures. As a writer, you approach one, bow, and then wait and see if it will bow in response. Only then do you know it's safe to climb aboard.

The Worst Sermon in History

The Bible tells of the worst sermon in history. The reason it's so abominable is that it's utterly devoid of metaphor. It's the sermon delivered by Jonah just after the great fish has vomited him up onto the beach. Chastened by his terrifying ordeal of divine disfavor, the reluctant prophet eventually does make his way to Ninevah, his assigned parish. Jonah walks the streets of the city, declaring, "Forty days more, and Nineveh shall be overthrown!" (Jonah 3:4).

That's it. That's Jonah's sermon: full manuscript. The problem is not that his message is dense with brain-clogging erudition. The smallest child could understand it. It's just completely unpersuasive. The sermon's utterly lacking in metaphor—unless the figure

5 Rowling, *Harry Potter and the Prisoner of Azkaban*, 115.

of Jonah, still dripping with the fish's digestive fluids, is himself a living metaphor.

So, what happens as a result of Jonah's grudging, slapdash sermon? God supercharges the prophet's half-hearted effort, saving the day. Incredibly, every last soul in Nineveh—instantly cut to the heart—dons sackcloth and repents with fasting. They even clothe their livestock in sackcloth.

No doubt the author is telling us this outcome is wholly God's doing. It certainly wasn't Jonah's poor excuse for a sermon that changed Ninevite hearts and minds. Barring extraordinary divine intervention, you need a few good metaphors to make that happen.

Follow the Drum Major

A good metaphor can drive an entire sermon. Such is the case with Martin Luther King Jr.'s famous sermon, "Drum Major Instinct."

It's an explication of Mark 10:35–45, in which Jesus rebukes his disciples James and John for trying to score prime seats in heaven. The driving metaphor of the sermon is the image of a drum major: that leader of a marching band who strides out ahead of the rest, pumping a baton, blowing a whistle, and generally saying, "Hey, everybody, look at me!"

Scholars who've studied the sermon diplomatically call it an adaptation of a sermon by another preacher whom King admired. That earlier sermon may have provided the drum major metaphor, but King adapts it to his own purposes—musing out loud whether his own activism has been an act of service or merely a ploy for attracting attention.

"We have some of the same James and John qualities," King honestly admits. "And there is deep down within all of us an instinct. It's a kind of drum major instinct—a desire to be out front, a desire to lead the parade, a desire to be first."[6]

---

6 Martin Luther King Jr., "The Drum Major Instinct," sermon delivered at the Ebenezer Baptist Church, Atlanta, GA, February 4, 1968, *Civil Rights Movement Archive*, https://www.crmvet.org/info/68mlkdrm.htm.

King reminds his listeners of Jesus's response to those overreaching disciples. He taught: "Whoever wishes to be first among you must be slave of all. For the Son of Man came not to be served but to serve, and to give his life a ransom for many" (Mark 10:44–45). This means, King continues:

> Everybody can be great, because everybody can serve. You don't have to have a college degree to serve. You don't have to make your subject and your verb agree to serve. You don't have to know about Plato and Aristotle to serve. You don't have to know Einstein's theory of relativity to serve. You don't have to know the second theory of thermodynamics in physics to serve. You only need a heart full of grace, a soul generated by love. And you can be that servant.[7]

King, of course, had no way of knowing the assassin's bullet would snatch away his own life just two months later. It's poignant to hear him in our imagination, musing about his own funeral, wondering what others might say about him on that day. All his honors and achievements—even his Nobel Peace Prize—are not what he wants remembered in his eulogy:

> Yes, if you want to say I was a drum major, say that I was a drum major for justice. Say that I was a drum major for peace. I was a drum major for righteousness. And all of the other shallow things will not matter. I won't have any money to leave behind. I won't have the fine and luxurious things of life to leave behind. But I just want to leave a committed life behind.[8]

There are other ways King could have said it, of course. He could have talked about Christian servanthood in the abstract. But that would have carried little rhetorical power. Everyone who's ever

---

7 King, "The Drum Major Instinct."

8 King, "The Drum Major Instinct."

witnessed an American football halftime show can picture the bold and brassy persona of the drum major, which in fairness to anyone who's ever taken up the baton and whistle, is not a character flaw but simply part of the role. The metaphor is homiletical gold. It gives shape to the entire sermon.

Where do we come up with great metaphors like the drum major? Wouldn't it be wonderful if there were some sort of machine that could help us create them? As it happens, one novelist has fantasized about that very thing.

Wishing for a Metaphor Machine

Umberto Eco's fantastical novel of the Baroque period, *The Island of the Day Before*, playfully addresses the question of where metaphors come from and how they function. Padre Emanuele—a character inspired by a Baroque philosopher of language, Emanuele Tesauro—stands beside the young Roberto, looking out over a landscape of farms. "What do you see, my boy?" "Fields," responds Roberto.[9]

Well, duh. He's answered correctly, the padre assures him. But there's so much more Roberto could have said about that idyllic landscape. Eco goes on, mimicking the florid writing style of the Baroque period:

> There, my son: if you had said simply that the Fields are pretty, you would have done nothing but depict for me their greening—which I already know of—but if you say the Fields laugh, you show me the earth as Animate. . . . And this is the office of the supreme figure of all: Metaphor. If Genius, & therefore Learning, consists in connecting remote Notions & finding Similitude in things dissimilar, then Metaphor, the most acute and farfetched among Tropes, is the only one capable of producing Wonder, which gives birth to Pleasure, as do

9 Umberto Eco, *Island of the Day Before* (HarperVia, 2006), 157–59.

> changes of scene in the theater. And if the Pleasure produced by Figures derives from learning new things, without effort & many things in small volume, then Metaphor, setting our mind to flying betwixt one Genus & another, allows us to discern in a single Word more than one Object.[10]

The next day, Padre Emanuele demonstrates an invention he calls his Aristotelian machine. Its purpose is to manufacture metaphors. Eco describes it as "the strangest imaginable piece of furniture . . . a great chest or case, whose front held eighty-one drawers—nine horizontal rows by nine vertical, each row in both directions identified by a carved letter."[11] On the top is a sort of lectern, displaying a large open book: an illuminated manuscript.

The machine consists of an array of rotating cylinders, each of which displays a variety of letters. A hand crank operates the machine, causing the cylinders "to revolve independently of one another, and when they stop, one could read triads of letters aligned at random."[12]

The letters refer to drawers in the lower part of the contraption. Each one contains a stack of parchment sheets with words written on them. Riffle through those stacks of sheets, and like some steampunk thesaurus, the machine delivers just the right metaphor.

Padre Emanuele's invention resembles an early mechanical calculator (a forerunner of the electronic computer), but this arcane device crunches words rather than numbers. The whole idea of such a machine is absurd, of course, but that's the point of the satire. Metaphors are wild and free, unconstrained by ordinary rules of logic. They're beyond the comprehension of the most advanced AI program but are readily accessible to children—at least, those above a certain age in their cognitive development—who delight in them.

---

10 Eco, *Island of the Day Before*, 157–59.

11 Eco, *Island of the Day Before*, 157–59.

12 Eco, *Island of the Day Before*, 157–59.

Metaphorical communication is an art, not a science. It's an art essential to good preaching.

But let's not give up on computers altogether. They do have a role to play in metaphor mongering. Although AI writing programs may deliver stock metaphors upon request, they're incapable of feeling the joy of comprehension, as an apt metaphor floods a complicated spiritual concept with light. What computers can do very well is efficiently file away metaphors and other material for future use, instantly retrieving them when asked. They can do this as long as you've already tagged that material with topic words that function like the letter triads of Padre Emanuele's machine.

Story: Engaging the Heart

Sitting beside Jacob's well in the Samaritan village of Sychar, Jesus looks up and sees a woman approaching, an empty clay water jar balanced on her head. The blazing noonday sun has driven everyone else from the streets. Ordinarily, Jews and Samaritans—with no love lost between them—would avoid conversation. But it's just the two of them there at the well. There's no avoiding the interaction.

Jesus asks her for a drink. She thinks his request strange: What does this crazy Jew want of me? But she complies readily enough.

The two speak of living water, which Jesus promises he can offer. How is that possible? What is this living water? This man is speaking of deeper, spiritual thirsts.

He seems to know her: not merely her outward circumstances but her inner life. This wandering rabbi is remarkably well informed about her complex marital history. Jesus doesn't reveal how her five previous marriages ended—By death? By divorce?—and her present living arrangement is clearly irregular. No doubt this water bearer has long been the target of village gossip. But she remains strong, feisty, and not at all reticent in talking theology with this foreigner.

Jesus is no shrinking violet either. He tells her a secret he hasn't even shared with his own disciples: He is the Messiah, whose coming Jews and Samaritans alike have long expected.

Thrilled by what she's hearing—and baffled, still, by all she doesn't yet understand—the Samaritan woman runs off to tell all her friends. "Come, and see a man who has told me all I have ever done!" (John 4:29).

Jesus has broken through her reserve. He's done it by telling her a story: in this instance, her own story. The Lord whom we proclaim is a world-class purveyor of stories.

Jesus's stories strike a chord with us because we human beings are what Jonathan Gottschall has called the storytelling animal:

> Tens of thousands of years ago, when the human mind was young and our numbers were few, we were telling one another stories. And now, tens of thousands of years later, when our species teems across the globe, most of us still hew strongly to myths about the origins of things, and we still thrill to an astonishing multitude of fictions on pages, on stages, and on screens—murder stories, sex stories, war stories, conspiracy stories, true stories and false. We are, as a species, addicted to story. Even when the body goes to sleep, the mind stays up all night, telling itself stories. . . . Human minds yield helplessly to the suction of story. No matter how hard we concentrate, no matter how deep we dig in our heels, we just can't resist the gravity of alternate worlds.[13]

Gottschall goes so far as to name our species "*Homo fictus* (fiction human), the great ape with the storytelling mind."[14] Although we may imagine that reading is "a passive act: we lie back and let writers pipe joy into our brains, [this conception] is wrong. When we experience a story, our minds are churning, working hard."[15] Writers (and, we could add, preachers) provide "expert line drawings with hints on

---

13 Jonathan Gottschall, *The Storytelling Animal* (Houghton Mifflon Harcourt, 2013), Preface, 3.

14 Gottschall, *The Storytelling Animal*, 136–37.

15 Gottschall, *The Storytelling Animal*, 136–37.

filling them in. [Readers'] minds supply most of the information in the scene—most of the color, shading, and texture."[16]

Although, in this wired world of ours, reading books is not nearly so common as it once was—people of our culture spend an astonishing amount of time gazing at images on screens—there's something about experiencing a story in the company of others that binds us together in community. Such is the traditional communal cinema experience, that in the age of Netflix, is growing increasingly rare:

> If the movie is good, the people will respond to it like a single organism. They will flinch together, gasp together, roar with laughter together, choke up together. A film takes a motley association of strangers and syncs them up. It choreographs how they feel and what they think, how fast their hearts beat, how hard they breathe, and how much they perspire. A film melds minds. It imposes emotional and psychic unity. Until the lights come up and the credits roll, a film makes people one. It has always been so. It is easy for us to forget, sitting alone on our couches with our novels and television shows, that until the past few centuries, story was always an intensely communal activity. For tens of thousands of years before the invention of writing, story happened only when a teller came together with listeners. It wasn't until the invention of the printing press that books became cheap enough to reward mass literacy. For uncounted millennia, story was exclusively oral. . . . Story, in other words, continues to fulfill its ancient function of binding society by reinforcing a set of common values and strengthening the ties of common culture.[17]

Long before Thomas Edison rolled out his first movie projector, the church was gathering on the Lord's Day to be wowed by a similar communal storytelling experience. They heard the story in God's

---

16 Gottschall, *The Storytelling Animal*, 136–37.

17 Gottschall, *The Storytelling Animal*, 136–37.

word proclaimed and saw it reenacted in the sacraments. Today's pulpit storytellers have a profusion of new electronic media to work with, but the minds of their congregations are still wired the same way. This means storytelling will always have a powerful role in the preaching event.

From our youngest days, stories enchant us. Preschoolers beg parents to read them bedtime stories. Many preliterate children are so tuned into story that they can recite their favorite picture books from memory. When two children come together with dolls or other toys, what's the first thing they do? They start crafting a story to cause their toys to interact. Buzz Lightyear and Barbie may seem an odd couple, but when the blond-haired beauty swoons for the chunky space ranger in his winged suit, differences of body type and circumstance aren't a deal-breaker. Such is the power of imagination.

In J. M. Barrie's *Peter Pan*, there's a scene when Peter is explaining to Wendy why he's been listening every night outside their nursery window. He's been eavesdropping on the stories Wendy's mother tells the children. "None of the lost boys knows any stories," Peter explains, sadly.[18]

Wendy responds sympathetically, whereupon she lets Peter fly her and her younger brothers through the air to Neverland where she can tell stories to the lost boys and tuck them in at night. The raging pandemic of unfounded conspiracy theories in our culture may be explained, in part, by an unsatisfied hunger for truly meaningful stories. Lacking such stories, the Proud Boys are revealed to be lost boys in Barrie's sense, vainly trying to satisfy soul hunger with narrative junk food.

Truly, we are all lost without stories. Keith Ablow, a forensic psychiatrist, has studied the motivations of those who attempt suicide. He told CNN's Larry King in a 2006 interview, "I think the thing that

---

18 James Matthew Barrie, *Peter and Wendy: Peter Pan, the Boy Who Wouldn't Grow Up* (Charles Scribner's Sons, 1911), chap. III, Project Gutenberg, https://www.gutenberg.org/ebooks/16.

binds together most people who go on to take their lives is that they have an inability to imagine the next chapter in their life stories."[19]

Christians come to church like expectant children anticipating their favorite tales. Adults, too, yearn to hear stories. And not just any stories. Our deepest yearning is for *the* story, the great story, the story of salvation history (note that the word *history* contains the word *story*).

The lilting strains of an old hymn—sadly omitted from many recent hymnals—captures the appeal for congregations, then as now:

Tell me the stories of Jesus
I love to hear;
Things I would ask him to tell me
If He were here:
Scenes by the wayside,
Tales of the sea,
Stories of Jesus,
Tell them to me.[20]

Embracing Your Inner Bard

An honored personage in ancient Celtic society was the bard. Bards were traveling storytellers and musicians. They captured the imagination of their listeners and instilled a sense of wonder. The stories they spun gave society cohesion and lifted the eyes of the people to see truths bigger than they could easily glimpse from their pastures, looms, and fishing boats. Although bards came and went among the people, they remained strangers in a deep sense. Itinerating from one village to another, they were in but not of the community. Chieftains hired the most gifted among them to take up more or less

19 *Larry King Live*, "Film About Suicide Opens in Theaters," *CNN*, October 27, 2006, transcript, https://transcripts.cnn.com/show/lkl/date/2006-10-27/segment/01.

20 William H. Parker, "Tell Me the Stories of Jesus," no. 204 in *Sunday School Hymnary*, ed. Carey Bonner (London: Sunday School Union, 1905), 218.

permanent residence in their banqueting halls—the bargain being that they would unceasingly sing the chieftain's praises. Then, as now, the bard's temptation is to forsake the call to speak truth to power.

Few church treasurers would readily admit it, but they're paying us, first and foremost, to be bards. Our people want us to spin tales of living water so refreshing to parched spirits they can almost taste it. More than that, after we've come to know our congregations, they expect us to reflect their own stories back to them, to help them recall everything they've ever done. This is the role played by a particular type of Irish storyteller, known as the *shanachie*. *Shanachies* were keepers of ancient family lineages like the genealogies of Jesus that begin two of the four Gospels. *Shanachies* were stewards of the collective memory of the people. Our job is to help God's people set their personal narrative inside the greater narrative of salvation: a story commodious enough to include, as principal characters, not only themselves but also a generous and loving God.

Theologian Henri Nouwen has wisely observed, "The discipline of the church is the discipline by which we remain in touch with the true story of God in history. . . . Without the Spirit, our upwardly mobile lives remain full but unfulfilled lives in which our many stories compete with each other for attention."[21]

In life—whether or not we're aware of it—we choose our own stories, the stories by which we live. We do well to ask ourselves what guiding stories we spend our lives writing, the stories others will one day repeat at our funeral. Are they stories of individual achievement? Of nurturing the next generation? Of conflict, competition, and triumph over enemies? Of unquestioning loyalty to an athletic team or nation? Of all-consuming love for hobbies, music, books, the great outdoors? More to the point, are they stories of faith?

Newspaper obituaries used to be formulaic exercises, conforming to a time-honored pattern. That was because obituaries used to be considered news articles. The obituary editor, ever-mindful of

---

21 Henri J. M. Nouwen, *The Selfless Way of Christ: Downward Mobility and the Spiritual Life* (Orbis, 2007), 71–76.

printing costs measured in column inches, was interested in little more than bare demographic facts: name, age, occupation, employment history, organizational affiliations, family connections, cause of death. There was a certain sameness from one obituary to the next: a boilerplate pattern into which the funeral director or next of kin would insert the distinctive details. Unless the deceased happened to be famous—a person of interest to the larger community of newspaper subscribers—most obituaries were composed of vital statistics and not much more. The person's true story was retold elsewhere, in a personal reflection or eulogy at the memorial service or over forkfuls of potato salad at the reception.

But all that changed when newspapers, both in print and online, started selling obituaries as though they were advertisements. That innovation has placed the survivors in the driver's seat. They've purchased the space, so they can share pretty much whatever they wish. And share they do—profusely, if they can afford to do so. Obituaries have become far more interesting reading than they used to be. They've become occasions for telling stories, stories that define the meaning of a human life.

True, we all have our own story and hope there's someone who knows it sufficiently well to polish it up and retell it after we've departed this earth. But far more significant, as Nouwen points out, is another story:

> Just as we only come to know our true selves by letting ourselves be known in and through Christ, so, too, can we only come to know the true events of our time in and through the story of Christ.
>
> The story of Christ is therefore not "the greatest story ever told," but the only story ever told. It is the story from which all other stories receive their meaning and significance. The story of Christ makes history real.[22]

---

22 Nouwen, *The Selfless Way of Christ*, 71–76.

It's *the only* story ever told. When you, as bard, illuminate a sermon—even though you're the author of the words you'll soon speak—you're doing far more than ornamenting your own creation, your own work of art. You're harmonizing with the only story, the great story, the true story: the story we find not in any single place in the Bible but throughout the Scriptures.

Early in our ministry, we learn how to properly tell our own story, the story of God's call in our lives. First, our supervising candidacy committees and, later, our parishioners, want to hear it. Throughout our ministry we learn to be storytellers—a few of those accounts being our own but most of them tales we've heard from others—stories that, in their faithful retelling, have power to lead people to Jesus Christ.

This is as it should be, because the gospel (it's called the good news, after all) is itself a story. If we are to be ministers of the gospel—servants of the word—a fundamental task is to learn the nuances of these lesser stories and how to retell them in order to acquaint our listeners with the truest of all stories.

Stories as Living-Water Jars

It's remarkable how little theology there is in the Bible, if we define theology as abstract teaching about the nature and attributes of God. To be sure, there's some explicit theology in the Hebrew wisdom literature and even more in the Pauline letters, but mostly what the Bible offers—apart from worship texts like the psalms—is story.

First-year divinity students quickly learn (if they don't know it already) that the Bible never mentions the Trinity. Partly that's because the historic ecumenical councils—abstracting the three-in-one Godhead from Scripture's overall witness—didn't fully articulate the doctrine until several centuries after the last New Testament authors had laid down their pens. But the principal reason why there's so little explicit theology in the Bible is because the Bible just doesn't work that way.

The greatest Christian doctrines are so deeply embedded in story that it's difficult to separate them from the narrative without rendering them incoherent. Take Jesus's resurrection, for instance. Preachers who enter the pulpit on Easter morning determined to rationally explain the resurrection are on a fool's errand. Quite apart from the many small factual discrepancies among the Gospels' narratives, the nature of the resurrection was a mystery even to those who witnessed it. It remains a mystery to this day. Theologians have labored mightily over the centuries to provide coherent explanations of, say, what a resurrection body is like, but their efforts have never risen above the level of fantasy. The best—and most peculiar—example comes from Augustine of Hippo. He declared that, in heaven, everyone will inhabit their thirty-year-old body (with height adjusted to a uniform standard for men and a corresponding shorter standard for women), healed from any disease or deformity from which they suffered in their earthly lives but with nonfunctioning genitals.[23]

Paul the apostle is too prudent to dash down such theological rabbit holes. He sticks to the story. In 1 Corinthians 15:3–8, he resolutely imparts the truth he has first received:

> That Christ died for our sins in accordance with the scriptures, and that he was buried, and that he was raised on the third day in accordance with the scriptures, and that he appeared to Cephas, then to the twelve. Then he appeared to more than five hundred brothers and sisters at one time, most of whom are still alive, though some have died. Then he appeared to James, then to all the apostles. Last of all, as to someone untimely born, he appeared also to me.

Paul doesn't seek to explain the resurrection. He simply shares the testimony of witnesses, both himself and others. The risen Christ

---

23 Aurelius Augustine, *City of God*, vol. 2, book 22, "Whether the bodies of all the dead shall rise the same size as the Lord's body," trans. Marcus Dods (T&T Clark, 1871), 15, 508.

appeared to them, and that's all he's got to say on the subject. It's his story and he's sticking to it. Far be it for us to do anything different.

Stories are not theology, but they often serve as containers for theology. They're like the clay water jar the Samaritan woman carries to the well. Jesus offers her living water but, curiously, says nothing of a vessel to hold it. Nor does he appear to have such a vessel. The Samaritan woman says as much: "Sir, you have no bucket and the well is deep." (John 4:11).

But then he tells her the story of all she ever did. In so doing, he's providing her with just such a container. The woman's testimony—the story she immediately shares with her neighbors—is the vessel. As we tell and retell sacred stories, we keep the living-water jar filled to the brim. If we do so faithfully, attentive listeners just may, by the power of the Spirit, be privileged to taste the living water Christ freely offers.

Poetry: The Beauty of Holiness

Poetry is a rich source of sermon illumination material—surprisingly so, because in modern times published poetry has an exclusive and vanishingly small fan base. In recent years, though, poetry's reputation among the younger generations, particularly younger people of color, has been growing dramatically but as live art rather than published poetry collections.

Quoting poetry in sermons is not about appealing to an avid fan base of poetry book enthusiasts. Such bookstore patrons do exist, but poetry is really an oral art form. The swiftest way to understand most poems is to read them aloud. For that reason, shorter poems or brief excerpts from longer ones are ideal for the oral art form that is preaching.

But you've got to do it well. To meaningfully share a poet's words takes careful preparation as well as practice. Techniques of oral interpretation are essential: phrasing, emphasis, emotional tone. As with Scripture readings, you must first exegete poetic texts before you can speak them with conviction and understanding.

If a poem is written in a recognizable meter, it's crucial to drill down deeper than the singsong rhythm of its lines. You've got to go behind the meter to discover its deep meaning and conversational rhythms. Focus on those conversational rhythms, even if it means ignoring commas, line breaks, and other signs that might otherwise lead you to robotically chant the poem as though it were a song.

Most poems benefit from being spoken as though they were prose. The meter is still there and will remain discernible to your listeners, but for you to speak in the poet's own voice—as though it were a one-on-one conversation—is all the more powerful.

The best Shakespearean actors know how to do this. Although Shakespeare wrote in both poetry and prose, the most noble of his characters' speeches are written in poetry, typically iambic pentameter. As a very simple example, consider these famous lines from *Henry V*, when the young king, sword in hand, rallies his soldiers to battle:

> Once more unto the breach, dear friends, once more;
> Or close the wall up with our English dead.[24]

Speaking these lines in strict iambic pentameter would sound like this (stressing the all-caps syllables):

> Once MORE unTO the BREACH, dear FRIENDS, once MORE
> or CLOSE the WALL up WITH our ENGlish DEAD.

That singsong rhythm sounds ridiculous. Who would follow a commander into battle who spoke like that? Yes, it's the way Shakespeare wrote it. But it's not the way he intended actors to speak it. Surely the bard intended a more conversational rhythm, something like this:

---

24 William Shakespeare, *The Life of Henry V*, ed. G. Blakemore Evans (Houghton Mifflin, 1974), 3.1.1–2.

ONCE MORE unto the BREACH, DEAR FRIENDS,
ONCE MORE
or CLOSE the WALL UP with our ENGLISH DEAD.

Yes, it's poetry. The iambic pentameter is still there, the depth structure beneath the surface. It won't be lost on your listeners. But you don't have to pound it with a rhetorical sledgehammer. Step into the role of the poet and speak those lines not as he wrote it but as he would likely read it, were he directing actors on the stage.

The music of poetry is more memorable than prose. Certainly, this was true of the huge media coverage given to Amanda Gorman's poem "The Hill We Climb," delivered at President Biden's inauguration. Her words made it into more newspapers and TV sound bites than most of the day's speeches, including the president's inaugural address. Shortly after that media exposure, two of Gorman's previously published books of poetry attained bestseller status.

According to the old three-points-and-a-poem homiletical cliché, poetry is little more than a bit of adornment, a final flourish prior to the closing prayer. The possibilities of using poetry throughout a sermon are far richer than that and are well worth exploring.

Quotations: Dispatches from the Communion of Saints

Besides metaphors, stories, and poems, the fourth type of material to prioritize in this storyboarding phase is quotations. These give voice not only to the preacher but to others as well, both living and dead. Not every quotation you may share comes from a Christian believer, but broadly speaking, these borrowed voices allow the congregation to hear from the communion of saints.

A few rules are worth citing.

First, if brevity is the soul of wit, this is even more true of quotations. Few things are more stultifying than reading aloud a lengthy chunk of someone else's writing. Within even the most ponderous paragraph, you can likely find a few lines worth highlighting: Zero in on them and skip the rest. Make generous use of ellipses

(. . .). Paraphrase whenever you can—remember, you're writing for speech, not composing an academic paper. Were you telling a friend about a magazine article you've just read, you wouldn't stand there and read the whole thing aloud. You'd summarize. The same economy of expression applies to quotations shared in sermons. Focus on communicating how those shimmering words first captured your attention and why you're eager for your people to have the same experience. Then share just enough to give them the flavor of it.

Second, be careful to source quotations accurately. Social media has spawned an epidemic of spurious quotations, satirized by the meme of a stern-looking President Lincoln sharing this public service announcement: Don't trust anything you read on the Internet. If a brief quotation lands in your social media feed sourced only by the name of the speaker, chances are good it's been maliciously altered, at best, or completely fabricated, at worst. Certain famous names (Albert Einstein, Winston Churchill, Mark Twain, to name a few) are particularly susceptible to such reputation abuse.

A notable example is the aphorism that the definition of insanity is doing the same thing over and over and expecting different results. It's frequently attributed to Albert Einstein, but you can also find citations pointing to Benjamin Franklin and others. None of them are correct. As documented in the misattributed list of Einstein quotations on Wikiquote, the earliest known occurrence—and probable origin—is from a 1981 publication of Narcotics Anonymous: "Insanity is using day after day knowing that only physical and mental destruction comes when we do."[25] Sourcing the quotation to Einstein may sound more authoritative than attributing it to some anonymous sage in a recovery group, but that doesn't make it correct. Carelessly citing misattributed quotations can, at best, call your scholarship into question. At worst, it can impugn your honesty.

Fortunately, there are ways to fact-check quotations like these—most notably, by searching within Wikiquote or Google Books for

25 Narcotics Anonymous, *Basic Text* (Narcotics Anonymous, 1981), 11.

documented citations. You may get pages of hits in response to your query, but keep drilling down until you find one that documents where and when it was spoken or written. You don't need to report the full citation in the body of your sermon. You just need to satisfy yourself that the quotation is real.

Third, be mindful of the character and reputation of the person you're quoting. Certain pop culture figures and entertainers may enjoy high name recognition and may say things that are witty or wise, but their names may have other connotations inconsistent with your message. Something similar can be true of religious leaders from non-Christian religious traditions. A quotation from the Dalai Lama or Ram Dass may perfectly mesh with your message, but it's important to clarify that this is a voice from another tradition. Quotations call forth a certain superpower, that of inviting another person to be a copreacher of your sermon. Just be aware that, in simply citing certain names with no further explanation, you may be getting more than you bargained for.

Metaphors are snapshots. Stories are movies. Poems are paintings. Quotations give voice to the communion of saints. All are potent techniques for illuminating a sermon.

CHAPTER SIX

The Exhibitor

Inviting Wonder

Some may think museum exhibitions are all about the artworks and artifacts on display. In fact, there's more to it than that. Curators get points for presentation as well as content. There's an art to mounting an exhibition. Having designed the special-exhibition gallery, the next task is to welcome museum patrons in.

Likewise, the shimmering stories and metaphors we've pulled out of our illumination archives—or recently discovered as part of our research—do more than simply ornament a predetermined outline. Sometimes they give shape to the design itself. The preacher's role at this point is as an exhibitor, one who uses the necessary skills to actually preach the sermon.

Preachers of my own Presbyterian tradition resonate with a phrase found in one of our classic mission statements, called "The Great Ends of the Church."[1] *Ends*, in this case, is a synonym for *purposes*. The first of these purposes—the proclamation of the gospel for the salvation of humankind—is clearly related to the church's preaching. But so is the sixth and final purpose, the exhibition of the kingdom of heaven to the world. For Jesus, who according to Mark 1:15, begins his

---

1 Constitution of the Presbyterian Church (U.S.A.), *The Book of Order*, vol. 2 (Office of the General Assembly, 2023), F-1.0304, 5.

ministry proclaiming the kingdom of God has come near, that sort of exhibition is the heart of his mission. Leaving behind his carpenter's tools, he takes to the roads of Galilee and Judea in order to exhibit the nearness of God's reign. Christ is the curator par excellence.

To exhibit something is to show it. To exhibit a sermon—to present it, live—is to preach it. The English word's Latin root (a compound of *ex-*, meaning "out," and *habere*, meaning "to hold") literally means "to hold out, to put on display." There's a specialized legal meaning as well: to present a significant piece of evidence in court (e.g., "Your Honor, allow me to present Exhibit A").

I once served on a jury for a murder trial. The prosecutor entered into evidence, as an exhibit, several crumpled bullets the coroner had surgically removed from the body of the murdered man. She delivered these grisly (but cleaned up) objects to us in pristine plastic evidence bags, asking us to pass them among ourselves.

There was no logical reason for her to do that. Yes, we'd dutifully watched and listened as she'd questioned a ballistics expert, but none of us had the training to draw forensic conclusions by handling those malformed lumps of lead. Her purpose was different. She wanted us to experience a faint echo of the emotional tempest the brutal act of violence had called forth. Sometimes telling is not enough. You've got to show as well.

The word *behold*—which occurs over fifteen hundred times in the Bible—was made for exhibition. In illuminating a theological truth, we don't so much explain it as shine a light upon it. "Behold," we say, beckoning our listeners. Come and see!

Author Annie Dillard advises writers not to hold back in sharing thrilling insights that spark imagination:

> One of the few things I know about writing is this: spend it all, shoot it, play it, lose it, all, right away, every time. Do not hoard what seems good for a later place in the book, or for another book; give it, give it all, give it now. The impulse to save something good for a better place later is the signal to spend it now. Something more will arise for later, something

> better. These things fill from behind, from beneath, like well water. Similarly, the impulse to keep to yourself what you have learned is not only shameful, it is destructive. Anything you do not give freely and abundantly becomes lost to you. You open your safe and find ashes.[2]

Her counsel is even more true for writers of sermons. There's a temptation to hoard your treasures out of sight in the museum warehouse, out of fear of running out. Even if that item is the last one in your database on that particular topic, Dillard's advice is to go for broke, to bet the bank on whatever hand of cards you may be holding—confident that new wonders will present themselves in successive hands.

What are your listeners seeking as they accept the exhibits you hand them, sealed in their plastic envelopes? What do they expect to accomplish, turning them over and over in their hands? Sure, they're looking for truth. But that's not all they're seeking. Even more than truth, they're seeking something *real*.

Wendell Berry's brilliant novel, *Jayber Crow*, contains a parable about a hunter who gets himself into a very tight spot. On a perfect fall day, this man is walking through the woods when he steps onto the wooden cover of an abandoned well that belonged to a long-forgotten homestead. The rotted wood gives way beneath his boots. He plunges into the watery depths below, comes up for air, and then grabs hold of the cool, mossy stones that line the side of the well.

Looking up, he sees a tiny circle of light, impossibly far away. There are no discernible handholds on the sides of the well. There's no point in calling out for help, because no one's nearby. Berry writes:

> How does this story end? Does he save himself? Is he athletic enough, maybe, to get his boots off and climb out, clawing with fingers and toes into the grudging holds between the rocks of the wall? Does he climb up and fall back? Does somebody, in

---

2 Annie Dillard, *The Writing Life* (Harper Perennial, 2013), 78–79.

fact, for a wonder, chance to pass nearby and hear him? Does he despair, give up, and drown? Does he, despairing, pray finally the first true prayer of his life?

Listen. There is a light that includes our darkness, a day that shines down even on the clouds. A man of faith believes that the Man in the Well is not lost. He does not believe this easily or without pain, but he believes it. His belief is a kind of knowledge beyond any way of knowing. He believes that the child in the womb is not lost, nor is the man whose work has come to nothing, nor is the old woman forsaken in a nursing home in California. He believes that those who make their bed in Hell are not lost, or those who dwell in the uttermost parts of the sea, or the lame man at Bethesda Pool, or Lazarus in the grave, or those who pray, "Eli, Eli, lama sabachthani."

Have mercy.[3]

In the all-embracing heart of God, no one is completely and irretrievably lost. This is the heart of Christian proclamation. The illuminations we share from the pulpit are solid handholds by which our listeners may pull themselves up and out of their peril.

TO BUILD A FIRE

This is not to say preaching begins and ends with mutely pointing out things that shimmer. You've got hard work ahead in the writing phase to bring listeners along with you on your intuitive journey. Preparing illuminations for actual use in a sermon is something like building a campfire.

Years ago, those of us who were Boy Scouts learned how to build a fire. For readers of older editions of the *Boy Scout Handbook*, that

3 Wendell Berry, *Jayber Crow* (Counterpoint, 2000), 356–57.

process began with memorizing a homey little rhyme by the naturalist Ernest Thompson Seton:

> First a curl of birch bark dry as it kin be,
> Then some twigs of softwood, dead, but on the tree,
> Last o' all, some pine-knots to make the kittle foam,
> An' thar's a fire to make you think
> you're settin' right at home.[4]

There's a natural progression to fire building. It involves a lot more than simply touching lit match to dry log. Striking the match is, in fact, the very last thing you do, as Thompson's rhyme suggests. Enshrined in that little stanza are several essential steps based on immutable natural laws, governing the gathering and sorting of different types of wood and then deploying them in just the right sequence.

First comes a curl of birch bark, among the most flammable of woodland materials. Like dry leaves, papery birch bark burns hot and fast, but its flame lasts a crucial few seconds longer than fallen leaves—just long enough to ignite a handful of very dry twigs, snapped off earlier from a tree and piled beside you, awaiting their moment. Those twigs, in turn, blaze hot enough to ignite a few finger-thick branches of kindling wood. Toss a few knots of sap-heavy pinewood into the burgeoning blaze, and before long, you can add thick hardwood logs. The ultimate goal is to grow your feeble flame until it puts out enough BTUs to make the water in that iron "kittle" foam.

It's essential to assemble the different types of wood ahead of time. You don't want to be caught flat-footed at the moment the fire's ready to be upgraded. If you have to dash around searching for what you need, the campfire will burn out in no time. Don't start writing a

---

4 Boy Scouts of America, *Boy Scout Handbook* (Boy Scouts of America, 1967), 177.

sermon without your homiletical woodpile close at hand. That's as pointless as going bowhunting without a quiver.

The point is, sermon illumination doesn't just happen. Your initial creative insight—the shimmer—does happen, and often unexpectedly, but it's got to be carefully shaped in subsequent stages in order to be serviceable.

A noted teacher of writing, George Saunders, describes this crucial rewriting stage—how it *really* works, not how we fancifully imagine our document springing to life fully formed:

> We often discuss art this way: the artist had something he wanted to express, and then he just, you know, expressed it. That is, we buy into some version of the intentional fallacy: the notion that art is about having a clear cut intention and then confidently executing same.
>
> The actual process, in my experience, is much more mysterious and beautiful and more of a pain in the ass to discuss truthfully.
>
> A guy (Stan) constructs a model railroad town in his basement. Stan acquires a small hobo, places him under a plastic railroad bridge, near that fake campfire, then notices that he's arranged his hobo into a certain posture—the hobo seems to be gazing back at the town. Why is he looking over there? At that little blue Victorian house? Stan notes a plastic woman in the window, then turns her a little, so she's gazing out. Over at the railroad bridge, actually. Huh. Suddenly, Stan has made a love story. (Oh, why can't they be together? If only "Little Jack" would just go home. To his wife. To "Linda.") What did Stan (the artist) just do? Well, first, surveying his little domain, he noticed which way his hobo was looking. Then he chose to change that little universe, by turning the plastic woman. Now, Stan didn't exactly decide to turn her. It might be more accurate to say that it occurred to him to do so—in a split second, with no accompanying language, except maybe a very quiet

internal "Yes." He just liked it better that way, for reasons he couldn't articulate, and before he'd had the time or inclination to articulate them. In my view, all art begins in that instant of intuitive preference.[5]

Continuing to labor over his writing, Saunders envisions a scientific meter, like a car's fuel gauge, mounted on his forehead. The meter's arrow swings between P (positive) and N (negative). The meter registers his feelings toward the words he's just written. Saunders explains:

> There's not an intellectual or analytical component to this; it's more of an impulse, one that results in a feeling of "Ah, yes, that's better." It's akin to that hobo adjustment, above: by instinct, in that moment.
>
> And really, that's about it. I go through the draft like that, marking it up, then go back and enter that round of changes, print it out, read it again, for as long as I still feel sharp—usually three or four times in a writing day. So: a repetitive, obsessive, iterative application of preference: watch the needle, adjust the prose, watch the needle, adjust the prose (lather, rinse, repeat), through (sometimes) hundreds of drafts, over months or even years. Over time, like a cruise ship slowly turning, the story will start to alter course via those thousands of incremental adjustments.[6]

Saunders is describing the art of fiction writing, but the art of sermon illumination—trading so heavily, as it does, in metaphor and story—functions in a similar way. You have to fuss with your text, through a series of small repetitive revisions, to get it ready for

---

5 George Saunders, *A Swim in a Pond in the Rain* (Random House, 2022), 110–11.

6 Saunders, *A Swim in a Pond in the Rain*, 111.

speech. This is true whether you're passing along a story someone else has created (say, in a newspaper article) or whether it's prose you've created out of whole cloth. Wherever it comes from, you have certain options in how you retell it. You have to convert the language that first shimmered for you into a conversational format that communicates that same shimmer from the pulpit. Through multiple revisions, you're looking to keep the come-and-see intact.

This is both a constructive and a destructive process, as a certain Yale undergraduate discovered to his dismay. He wrote a letter to one of his professors, the famed poet A. E. Housman, asking the master how he always managed to choose the right word. Housman responded acerbically: "I do not choose the right word. I get rid of the wrong one."[7]

Sometimes it's hard to let go of the first-draft language, but it has to be done. You can't say "in with the new" unless you first say, "out with the old." Or, as the British writer Arthur Quiller-Couch famously advised, you've got to learn how to "murder your darlings."[8]

Writing teacher William Zinsser puts it bluntly:

> Rewriting is the essence of writing well: it's where the game is won or lost. That idea is hard to accept. We all have an emotional equity in our first draft; we can't believe that it wasn't born perfect. But the odds are close to 100 percent that it wasn't.[9]

This is an especially tough concept for preachers to grasp. We believe we've been called by God to do what we do, and we call on the Holy Spirit for inspiration as we fine-tune our language. But we've got to believe the Spirit guides us not just at the thrilling moment

---

7 Floyd C. Watkins et al., *Talking with Robert Penn Warren* (University of Georgia Press, 1990), 116.

8 Arthur Quiller-Couch, *On the Art of Writing: Lectures Delivered in the University of Cambridge, 1913–1914* (Cambridge University Press, 1916), XII. On Style.

9 William Zinsser, *On Writing Well: An Informal Guide to Writing Nonfiction*, 30th anniv. edn. (Harper Perennial, 2016), 1,194, Kindle.

when we discover the shimmer but throughout the tedium of the revision process.

How a Kite String Becomes a Bridge

Humorist Garrison Keillor tells the story of how the first railway suspension bridge was constructed over the Niagara River in 1855, connecting the twin communities of Niagara Falls, Ontario, and Niagara Falls, New York. Constructing this first-of-its-kind wooden bridge was an engineering feat that could only be accomplished by an incremental approach:

> Before the bridge, people crossed the river by boat, mostly the tourist vessel *Maid of the Mist*, which traveled right up to the falls, giving its passengers an eyeful of natural beauty. Most people scoffed at the idea of a bridge, especially one that could support a train. An engineer named Charles Ellet Jr., a rather dramatic personage with a flair for showmanship, developed some interesting ideas for attaching a line across the tremendous gorge that involved firing cannonballs and rockets.
>
> He settled for a contest—he offered $5.00 to any boy who could fly a kite across the gap from the Canadian side and tie the kite string on the American side. Streams of young boys attempted the feat. One boy accomplished it after a few days, and Ellet's men tied a heavier line to the kite string and pulled a line across the gap, continuing to do so with heavier and heavier lines. In 1848 Ellet became the first person to cross the gorge by bridge when he went across in a basket. Later, he made the trip in his horse-buggy, standing like a gladiator. The bridge was 250 feet above the water.
>
> By 1860, more than 45 trains traveled the bridge each day.[10]

10 Garrison Keillor, *The Writer's Almanac for March 8, 2021*, March 8, 2021, transcript and audio, https://www.garrisonkeillor.com/radio/twa-the-writers-almanac-for-march-8-2021/.

Ellet's temporary span—ultimately expanded and completed by the famed engineer John Augustus Roebling, who added a lower deck for horse cart and pedestrian traffic—revolutionized travel and commerce between the two countries. Among other functions, it served as the final leg of the Underground Railroad for fugitive slaves, who snuck across its lower span by night.

It all began with a boy and his kite string. But the bridge could never have grown to support a railway train without that meticulous process of revision, pulling progressively stronger cables across the surging river. Great sermons may begin with a high-flying idea, but they're not ready for prime time without re-reading, correcting, and expanding over the course of many revisions.

King Tut Conquers New York

A few days before Thanksgiving 1976, the doors of New York's Metropolitan Museum of Art (the Met) opened for a special exhibition unlike any that museum-rich city—or the nation—had ever seen. *Treasures of Tutankhamun* would run for nearly a year to sellout crowds. Over eight million visitors would ultimately walk through the Met's special gallery, gawking at Egyptian gold. After the exhibit's long Manhattan run finally ended, King Tut's next-worldly possessions went on the road for a two-year, nationwide tour of other American museums, captivating another eight million visitors. After his US triumph, the boy king's roadshow continued to shatter attendance records at six other notable museums in Canada and Europe.

The Met's curators brilliantly exploited the confluence of several unique factors. A diplomatic rapprochement between the United States and Egypt allowed the pharaoh's gold burial mask and an assortment of his lamps, jars, daggers, jewelry, furniture, musical instruments, and gilded wood figurines to cross the Atlantic for the first time. Images from Howard Carter's 1922 excavation—printed from the Met's own collection of photographic plates—could now be paired with some of the actual items he'd unearthed. The spooky backstory of the excavation, including fanciful tales of King Tut's curse, added to the mystique.

The curators knew the exhibition was going to be a blockbuster, so they planned for overflow crowds. They sold special-admission tickets printed with entry times. They plastered New York's buses and subway cars with posters of the gold burial mask. The news media lapped it up, making it a national story. On TV's *Saturday Night Live*, comedian Steve Martin pranced across the stage in a Broadway-style musical number, costumed as an exuberant version of the boy king (in real life, King Tut was a sickly product of royal inbreeding who died young).

It seemed astonishing that all this fuss was over an exhibition of three-thousand-year-old artifacts. As a historical figure, this pharaoh was utterly forgettable. He reigned for less than two years—the last of his line—and died at age eighteen. The only reason he's so famous is the happy accident that grave robbers never plundered his tomb. Before King Tut's hoard blew into New York, museum Egyptology sections had been a backwater. Suddenly, not only mummy cases but also museums themselves were sexy.

It just goes to show what a great exhibition design can do.

I can remember visiting that exhibit as a teenager. The exhibit space was darkened and its succession of small rooms artfully illuminated by track lighting. Ingeniously placed wall partitions expedited traffic flow. The exhibition's signature artifacts were placed in prominent, spotlit locations, visible from a distance. This encouraged the crowd to keep moving, drawn on by what was coming next. Explanatory placards were succinctly written, offering just enough information to inform but not overwhelm. Of course, everyone exited into a special gift shop to browse a selection of books and curios suitable for any budget. There was no doubt about the expected outcome: Having seen all that gold, we were invited to part with a little of our own.

The curators gave pride of place to the most famous artifact in the exhibition: King Tut's gold burial mask. This was the image that had been blazoned on all the exhibition's advertising. The gallery design did not disappoint: The burial mask was placed on a pedestal in a darkened room, the focal point of numerous spotlight beams.

Crucially important to curation is this aspect of gallery design. Museum curators need to consider the number and variety of people who will pass through, configuring the rooms to channel traffic effectively.

Sermons are more like special exhibitions than permanent galleries. In permanent galleries, museumgoers wander at will. They're welcome to proceed at their own pace. Some pull out a pad and sketch. Others spend long minutes, even hours, deeply contemplating a single artwork. Still others surreptitiously practice the art of people-watching. It's all very free-form and permissive.

Not so with special exhibitions. A cohort of patrons marches through the gallery together, at a similar pace. In designing a sermon, you the preacher curate your listeners' experience in advance. Together you'll progress through a series of encounters with various artifacts: exegesis, commentary, quotations, metaphor, story, to name a few. Those artifacts may be displayed in any order. There's no one-size-fits-all design. Each sermon—like each special exhibition—must be imagined anew, based on the array of objects assembled for the occasion.

There may be explanatory material for museumgoers to read, printed on small placards or lettered in calligraphy on the walls. Or not: Sometimes a Craddock-style minimalist approach works best, inviting patrons to draw their own conclusions. Some artifacts must be explained to be understood. Others speak powerfully for themselves. Unlike a lecture—which is all about imparting information—a creatively written sermon, like a day at the museum, is a multisensory experience.

In recent years, technology has made this literally true. The screens commonly found in many sanctuaries have expanded the range of worshipers' sensory experiences. Visual imagery, in particular, can be a powerful addition to standard verbal testimony, especially for the visual learners among us. But there are pitfalls here. Presentation software programs like PowerPoint make it all too easy to deluge a congregation with cheesy stock-photo images of sunsets and smiling people or overengineered subscription video clips reminiscent of TV commercials. The distance from seat to screen—or, for online participants, from the eyes to the small screen of a tablet or smartphone—may blur the subtleties of even the best image or video.

Conventional verbal illuminations, carefully constructed and shared using concrete, sensory language, can ignite the imagination just as effectively. We see with our brains as much as our eyes. At the end of the day, it's imagination that sparks the magic. It matters not whether words or projected images conjure that genie.

That great artisan of imagination, Walt Disney, famously said, "Every child is born blessed with a vivid imagination. But just as a muscle grows flabby with disuse, so the bright imagination of a child pales in later years if [they cease] to exercise it."[11] An artfully designed sermon sparks holy imagination for all God's children, of whatever age.

Imaginative design rarely leads people in a straight-line fashion. It's full of surprises, as we'll see next.

THE KNIGHT'S MOVE

Preaching is persuasive speech. Your purpose in stepping into the pulpit is not merely to inform but also to motivate. Just as you've been called to ministry, your task in every sermon is to issue a call in miniature, inviting listeners to consider anew how God may be calling them to a different way of living.

Not every sermon, of course, must conclude with a formulaic call to discipleship, an impassioned invitation to make a decision for Christ. In some Christian traditions, each and every sermon does conclude with an altar call. I've even seen this happen at a graveside service. But the reality is that few, if any, listeners in a typical Sunday gathering are completely naive to the gospel. In much of

11 Dave Smith, ed., *The Quotable Walt Disney* (Disney Editions, 2001), 134.

the evangelical tradition, the altar call aspires to be an evangelistic vehicle, but it actually functions as a quasi sacrament for the already convinced. It's more a remembrance and renewal of each disciple's historic decision than a practical means by which the Lord daily "adds to their number those who [are] being saved" (Acts 2:47).

Most Sunday sermons preach to the choir to some degree, but that doesn't mean those proverbial choir members have no need of encouragement. Christian discipleship is a lifelong pattern of call and response. Numerous decision points rise up along life's journey. Preaching is meant to persuade believers and nonbelievers alike, in ways large and small, that "now is the acceptable time; see, now is the day of salvation" (2 Cor 6:2).

From Aristotle onward, rhetoricians have sought to identify and display the basic elements of persuasive speech. In terms of their general function, a great many of these elements operate in a way analogous to the knight's move in chess.

Recall that, in that game, the knight is the one piece that moves in a direction other than a straight line. Its irregular, L-shaped pattern evokes a mounted knight's leap over a foot soldier. In sermons, many persuasive techniques mimic the knight's move. These persuasive moves briefly depart from the forward momentum of the argument, moving to the side before returning again. These marginal spaces are where some of the most memorable insight happens.

No doubt you've noticed a number of knight's moves as you've read this book. I've done that on purpose, jumping from theoretical text to story to poem to quotation and back again to the main argument multiple times. I've studded the text with metaphors. I've changed it up. I've kept it fresh. I've done that partially as a demonstration of illumination technique, but more than that, I've done it to keep you reading. I've done it because it works.

The rhetorical knight's move is not unique to preaching. One of today's most effective practitioners is MSNBC journalist Rachel Maddow, who consistently garners some of the highest viewer ratings in television. She typically begins each program with an extended historical anecdote describing a situation that parallels some hot topic in the news. These anecdotes are long, sometimes as long as one-quarter of her hour-long broadcast.

But where does she find her material, in the pressure-cooker atmosphere of a TV newsroom? Maddow's colleague Chris Hayes was interviewing her at a special televised town-hall event featuring audience questions. He read a question from an audience member, a very pointed, practical question about how Maddow finds her material: "How do you come up with such amazing topics that start being totally random and drive a stake through the heart of a relevant event?" This fan is describing a standard Maddow move: starting with a jocular, meandering retelling of some historical anecdote that seems at first to be a shaggy-dog story but which eventually delivers viewers right to the doorstep of that day's headlines.

Maddow began her reply with a standard homage to the importance of being well read. Then—prodded by her colleague to get more specific—she quickly got down to brass tacks about how she finds illumination material on short notice:

> In general, it's good to read all the time. . . . Read beyond the assigned reading . . . Read stuff that interests you. . . . The way that this works on a day-to-day basis is that there's something going on out there in the news that I . . . want to understand better, and I just keep looking stuff up about it until I find something that interests me, and then I teach myself that thing, and then I teach other people that thing. . . . If you don't mind coming along on the journey that I'm on, I really believe that over the course of one conversation, you can get to a graduate school level of complexity with anybody, as long as you're willing to start together in kindergarten. . . . By the time we get to the end of the story, I want you to understand it well enough that you can tell somebody else. Not just send the clip of Rachel doing it, but so that *you* can do it . . . that you can tell that story.[12]

12 *Why Is This Happening? Live with Chris Hayes and Rachel Maddow*, MSNBC, December 22, 2023. Transcribed from recorded broadcast.

There are several lessons in this TV journalist's words that apply to preaching. First, note Maddow's emphasis on finding tangential stories that interest her. That's another way of saying she's looking for the shimmer. She's not afraid to deviate from the laser-focused pursuit of that day's topic if a knight's move takes her someplace interesting—as long as she can eventually find her way back again. Second, it's an educational process for her as well as her viewers: "I teach myself that thing, and then I teach other people that thing." Her style is to share her own joy of discovery, inviting her viewers on a shared journey. Third, she wants to share her knight's-move illuminations in such a way that the readers not only hear and appreciate her anecdotes but also internalize them so that, if called upon, they can share the stories themselves.

Maddow goes on to address the subject of repetition, the distinctive way she has of telling one aspect of a story and then repeating it, looping back around and repeating some story elements multiple times. She acknowledges that some of her viewers get frustrated with how much repetition she builds into her retelling. They ask her why she needs to tell them something, then tell them again, and then tell them that she's told them. But Rachel sticks to her guns. She makes it clear that this kindergarten teacher's pedagogy is very intentional. It's the repetition that helps the details of the story sink in.

What Maddow is describing here is a sort of live, in-the-moment curation process, one that's useful for times when there isn't a perfect story waiting in the database. She takes full advantage of hypertext links and source citations embedded in internet articles, letting her curiosity lead her into sideways, knight's-move leaps into new territory. Eventually, she happens upon a story she hasn't heard before—or perhaps has forgotten about—one that offers uncanny parallels to her current-events topic du jour. It's one reason why she's got so many fans.

This may sound like more of a journalism technique than one appropriate to preaching, but remember that preaching is, after all, about sharing good news. As a preacher, you're a journalist of the gospel, a peddler of stories that invite listeners to leap onto their own horse and risk executing the knight's move in tandem with you. If you need to swing your head around a time or two and ask your people "Are you with me?," that's all part of the game. It's a journey you take together.

Persuasive Communication

Social psychologists—some doubtless working for the advertising industry—have exhaustively studied the nature of persuasive communication. One notable pair of researchers, Richard E. Petty of Ohio State University and John T. Cacioppo of the University of Chicago, maintains that there are two routes to persuasion. There is a central route: the shortest route from point A to point B, which makes use of rational reflection and argument. But there's also what they call the peripheral route, which deviates from the argument's predictable logical path. It's a pathway "based on affective associations or simple inferences tied to peripheral cues."[13] This is not to say the peripheral route is illogical; it's more accurate to say it's alogical, in that it relies on emotional and aesthetic motivators to bring listeners to the same place they would otherwise have ended up had they followed the rational method alone.

Neuroscientists Francesca M. M. Citron and Adele E. Goldberg conducted a revealing study of how metaphorical language is more emotionally engaging than literal language. Even changing one word can make a difference. These researchers learned, for example, that their experimental subjects rated the line "She looked at him sweetly" as more emotionally engaging than "She looked at him kindly." Logically, there's little difference between the two expressions. Both convey benevolence or affection. Yet, the word *sweetly* is

---

13 Richard E. Petty and John T. Cacioppo, "The Elaboration Likelihood Model of Persuasion," *Advances in Experimental Social Psychology* 19 (December 1986): 191, https://www.sciencedirect.com/science/article/abs/pii/S0065260108602142.

metaphorical. Sweetness belongs to the sense of taste rather than the sense of vision, requiring listeners to join the speaker in a knight's-move metaphorical leap—something not required to understand how a look could be kind.[14]

The metaphors we choose do make a difference. In one psychological study, researchers Stephen J. Flusberg, Teenie Matlock, and Paul H. Thibodeau asked a group of experimental subjects to read a brief article on climate change.[15] Then they divided their subjects into two groups, presenting each cohort with a different metaphor to inspire them to action. The first cohort was asked to join a "war" on climate change. The appeal was freighted with emotionally charged military language ("The entire country should be recruited to fight this deadly battle"). The second cohort was urged to take the same actions, but the appeal this time was in terms of a footrace ("The entire country needs to step up to the line and get in front of this challenging problem"). Not surprisingly, the war cohort reported a higher level of engagement. The researchers describe the lower-intensity response of the footrace group:

> This metaphor still captures the idea of a competition with winners and losers, but it lacks the emotional intensity of war. The results showed that the war metaphors made people feel a greater sense of risk and urgency about the threat from climate change, leading them to express a greater willingness to engage in various conservation behaviors.[16]

---

14 Francesca M. M. Citron and Adele E. Goldberg, "Metaphorical Sentences are More Emotionally Engaging Than Their Literal Counterparts," *Journal of Cognitive Neuroscience* 26, no. 11 (November 2014): 2585–95, https://pubmed.ncbi.nlm.nih.gov/24800628/.

15 Stephen J. Flusberg et al., "Metaphors for the War (or Race) Against Climate Change," *Environmental Communication* 11, no. 6 (November 2017): 769–83, https://doi.org/10.1080/17524032.2017.1289111.

16 Paul H. Thibodeau and Stephen J. Flusberg, "Metaphors in Persuasive Communications," *Medium*, December 24, 2021, https://medium.com/bending-the-arc/metaphors-in-persuasive-communications-6d714849f403.

There's a reason political leaders frequently rely on military metaphors (the war on poverty, the war on cancer). Such images stir up complex feelings of fear and anger in a way other metaphors do not. All of us are more in thrall to our emotions than we'd care to admit.

Tell It Slant

One of Emily Dickinson's most baffling—but also most engaging—poems is this one:

Tell all the truth but tell it slant—
Success in Circuit lies
Too bright for our infirm Delight
The Truth's superb surprise
As Lightning to the Children eased
With explanation kind
The Truth must dazzle gradually
Or every man be blind—[17]

In a few brief lines, Dickinson captures the persuasive beauty of metaphor in poetry, which we can easily extend to the more poetic aspects of preaching. Yes, the essence of preaching is truth telling, but a straightforward theological explanation, plucked from Bible commentaries or systematic theology textbooks, is often too dazzling to take in. Success, therefore, lies in circuit (the knight's move, the spiraling homiletical helix), inviting listeners, by means of story and imagery, to discover and delight in shimmering surprises. At times, holy light manifests itself more intensely than a mere shimmer, so a kind explanation is much appreciated, for "God's lightnings light up the world; the earth sees and trembles" (Ps 97:4). But explanations are never the main purpose. The function

17 Ralph W. Franklin, ed., *The Poems of Emily Dickinson: Reading Edition* (Harvard, 1998), poem no. 1263.

of metaphor in preaching—telling it slant—is to enable God's truth to dazzle gradually.

We've noted how, in many Christian traditions, pastors are the product of graduate theological education, which means they've spent long years perfecting the persuasive writing methods of the academy. Those methods tend to honor the central, rather than the peripheral, route to persuasion. In many academic disciplines—especially the heritage theological disciplines of biblical studies, systematic theology, and church history—peripheral arguments are at best irrelevant and at worst actively discouraged. We've observed how so many seminarians land in the preaching classroom urgently needing to unlearn certain research and writing techniques they've spent years honing. Some never succeed in making the shift. Their sermons sound more like exegesis papers than persuasive proclamation.

One day, when my wife, Claire, and I were young parents, our daughter, Ania, developed serious cold symptoms. She had a history of painful ear infections, so we were concerned. We took her to the pediatrician, who after examining her, solemnly delivered his diagnosis: purulent rhinitis.

We were aghast. What loathsome disorder was this?

Then I looked at the doctor. He had a twinkle in his eye. "It means a runny nose," he explained kindly. He prescribed some over-the-counter medication, and we were on our way, much relieved.

Sometimes it doesn't occur to us who've spent considerable time and treasure pursuing graduate theological education how stubbornly our beloved twenty-dollar theological terms can impede meaningful communication. Other professions, such as law and medicine, have their own arcane vocabularies, but these are intended as insider language for expert practitioners. Neither a defendant in a courtroom nor a patient on an operating table needs to master the rarified vocabulary. That's for the professionals to worry about. It's different for us when we step into the pulpit. Our task is not theology but proclamation. Our people count on us to manifest the Pentecostal charism from Acts 2:11 so that they, too, may marvel, "In our own languages we hear them speaking about God's deeds of power."

It's not uncommon to hear pastoral search committee members say they're looking for candidates who don't simply read their sermons—in the way a professor presents a paper at a scholarly conference. By this, they mean they're looking for polished public speakers who maintain a conversational tone, using eye contact and body language effectively. These are not difficult skills to learn, but (reading between the lines) the search committee is also looking for something else. They're looking for communicators adept at a particular way of *writing* the sermon, not merely delivering it. They mistakenly assume that speaking off the cuff is the only way to achieve a conversational style. They hunger for the sort of peripheral arguments that are the bane of the academy. They're seeking a plain-speaking preacher who knows how to tell the truth but to tell it slant.

This isn't simply a matter of abandoning a sermon manuscript for notes or an outline. The notes-versus-manuscript debate will likely never be resolved. The truth is, even a noteless preacher can deliver a straight-down-the-middle academic discourse burdened with pedestrian language and devoid of illumination. Conversely, a manuscript preacher—far from simply droning on like a bookish don at some scholarly conclave—can, by means of careful preparation and at least partial memorization, present a lively and engaging message. Indeed, many of history's most notable preachers have used precisely that technique. The crucial factor is not what sort of physical text, be it paper or electronic tablet, rests before them on the pulpit but what sort of content that source contains. Does the message invite listeners' engagement by means of story and metaphor, or does it demand they do all the intellectual labor of connecting theology to their daily lives?

TRUST YOUR PERIPHERAL VISION

The poet Robert Frost tells the tale of an odd New England character named Brad McLaughlin, an amateur astronomer:

So Brad McLaughlin mingled reckless talk
Of heavenly stars with hugger-mugger farming,
Till, having failed at hugger-mugger farming,
He burned his house down for the fire insurance
And spent the proceeds on a telescope
To satisfy a lifelong curiosity
About our place among the infinities. . . .
He had been heard to say by several:
"The best thing that we're put here for's to see;
The strongest thing that's given to us to see with's
A telescope. Someone in every town
Seems to me owes it to the town to keep one.
In Littleton it may as well be me."[18]

Old Brad is a quirky small-town character—and his ethics in torching his farmhouse for insurance money surely aren't the best—but he's driven by a passion symbolic of noble human aspiration: the desire to see. Brad's right about one thing: Someone in every town, preoccupied with discovering "our place among the infinities,"[19] ought to keep a telescope:

Often he bid me come and have a look
Up the brass barrel, velvet black inside,
At a star quaking in the other end.
I recollect a night of broken clouds
And underfoot snow melted down to ice,
And melting further in the wind to mud.
Bradford and I had out the telescope.
We spread our two legs as it spread its three,
Pointed our thoughts the way we pointed it,
And standing at our leisure till the day broke,

---

18 Robert Frost, "The Star-Splitter," in *New Hampshire* (Henry Holt, 1923), 27.

19 Frost, "The Star-Splitter," 27.

Said some of the best things we ever said.
That telescope was christened the Star-Splitter,
Because it didn't do a thing but split
A star in two or three the way you split
A globule of quicksilver in your hand
With one stroke of your finger in the middle.
It's a star-splitter if there ever was one,
And ought to do some good if splitting stars
'Sa thing to be compared with splitting wood.[20]

Keeping a telescope is what preachers do. We practice the fine art of seeing, splitting stars as Brad McLaughlin did. What we observe of the infinities, of course, is rarely so well defined as what shows up in a telescope's eyepiece. It's a matter of peripheral vision: not locating fixed constellations but marveling at the here-today-gone-tomorrow manifestation, the shooting star tracing its bright path across the sky. Unlike scientists, whose time-honored method demands reproducible results, we preachers learn to trust our fleeting peripheral vision. We trade in holy rumors. We spin tales of truths that can't be replicated in the laboratory.

We long for the shooting star. We seek the shimmer. Once we're blessed with the vision, however fragile, we find creative ways to describe the ephemeral God-sighting to others. The light we borrow is celestial. We deploy writers' tools, story and metaphor, to point others to the bright wonder as it appears in their own lives.

Glamour: Transformative Magic

It's work that's got a certain glamour to it. By glamour, I don't mean the usual way that word's used today. It's got a much older meaning.

In modern usage, glamour describes artfully fabricated beauty. There used to be a popular print magazine with that very name, a Condé Nast publication that lives on in electronic form. Its

20 Frost, "The Star-Splitter."

original name was *Glamour of Hollywood*. It purveyed to small-town women tips and tricks for mimicking their movie-star idols: cosmetics, fashion, and similar artifice. The name was soon shortened to simply *Glamour*, but fascination with Hollywood is still what it's all about.

Originally, glamour had a broader meaning, with supernatural overtones. Glamour meant transformation: a shape-shifting change from one form into another. Glamour was a supernatural power exercised by the likes of Merlin, friend and mentor to King Arthur. It's said Merlin could transform himself into various woodland animals and back again.

Glamour is enchantment. It's magic: not the glitzy Hollywood alchemy of rouge, eyeshadow, and designer gowns but the imaginative transformation of one thing into another.

Every time we, as preachers, stand before a congregation, we're seeking to be glamourous in the most ancient sense of the word. Not "Mr. DeMille, I'm ready for my close-up" glamorous, but we do seek to artfully apply creative power to change reality for the better. One megachurch promoted itself with the tagline "Come as you are, leave as you want to be." As glib as that slogan may sound, it's not so far off from the experience every church aspires to offer. "Come join us, and you'll be a better person for it; depart with us, and the world will be better because of the ways we serve neighbors together in Christ's name."

Glamour is what happens when we, as pulpit writers, unleash the power of metaphor. Unlike similes—which, using the modifier *like*, merely compare one thing to another—metaphors imaginatively and unapologetically transform one thing into another.

It's not a straightforward process. There's a sort of fuzzy logic to the way metaphors work. We know we're supposed to avoid mixing them, but apart from that, there are few rules.

"O my luve is like a red red rose," sings the poet Robert Burns in the Scots dialect, beginning one of his most famous poems with a simile. But he later steps over from simile into metaphor:

Till a' the seas gang dry, my dear,
And the rocks melt wi' the sun;
I will luve thee still, my dear,
While the sands o' life shall run.[21]

The poet doesn't claim long-lasting affection like the earth's geological processes. He simply says, "Till a' the seas gang dry."[22] Burns's imagery is reminiscent of the psalmist who defiantly promises, "Therefore we will not fear, though the earth should change, though the mountains shake in the heart of the sea" (Ps 46:2). There's no *like* there, no logical placeholder signaling a mere simile that's an intellectual construct, nothing more. Pull out that stop, as a pulpit writer, and you invite listeners to throw caution to the wind and imaginatively experience metaphorical shape-shifting: to wonder at the glamour.

Much of what preachers do in the pulpit aspires to be transformational in that way. We don't seek merely to help our people think about what life was like in Jesus's day. We want to put a robe and sandals on them. Our goal is not unlike that old spiritual song "I Walked Today Where Jesus Walked," the anthem of Holy Land pilgrims, whose first stanza speaks of slowly and reverently wandering down the same paths Jesus walked and feeling his presence there.[23]

Reminding our listeners of Isaiah's call in the temple, preachers want the fragrant scent of incense to invade their people's nostrils, the sizzling coal clasped in the seraph's tongs to warm their lips. Relating the Samaritan's tender care of the man who fell among thieves, we hope their fingers will sense the reassuring tightness of the well-wrapped bandage, the weighty promise of the silver coin they place in the innkeeper's palm. Recalling the track of a single tear down Mary Magdalene's cheek, we wish that all who have known

21 Robert Burns, "A Red, Red, Rose," in *Selected Poems* (Penguin, 1994), 178.

22 Burns, "A Red, Red, Rose," 178.

23 "I Walked Today Where Jesus Walked," text by Daniel S. Twohig (G. Schirmer, 1937).

grief may reexperience that salty taste before being astounded, amid an unexpected embrace, at how love lives on.

Isn't that why people forsake all the other attractions of a Sunday morning and turn their attention—at least for the first minute or two, and longer if we do it right—to what we have to say? They long for shape-shifting glamour. They want to see their daily labors as noble, their marriages as holy, their government as redeemable, their sins as curable. They yearn to believe that somewhere, not so very far down their personal Damascus Road, they will encounter an intersection where a turning is not only possible but also likely if they attend to the voice calling their name.

And then, sealing the deal—if it's a Sunday when we're celebrating the Lord's Supper—we step down from the pulpit and over to the table, where we utter the greatest shape-shifting words of all: "This is my body . . . this is my blood."

Similes have their place. But when it comes to calling forth real change, there's nothing so glamorous as metaphor.

PLAYING LANGUAGE GAMES

There's no one-size-fits-all when it comes to sermon design. No two Scripture texts or sermon topics—or two congregations—are alike. You tailor your design to your material and to your audience.

Ludwig Wittgenstein was one of the great philosophers of language of the early twentieth century. Having studied engineering in his native Austria, he became enthralled by the philosophy of mathematics. On a tip from one of his professors, he journeyed to the University of Cambridge, seeking to study under the renowned Bertrand Russell. The Cambridge don was impressed by the soaring intellect of this intense young man who'd literally walked up to his door one day and knocked. Russell would later declare him the most brilliant student he'd ever taught.

Wittgenstein's landmark philosophical work is the short but incredibly dense *Tractatus Logico-Philosophicus*, in which he seeks to discern, in the workings of language, the meaning and significance of all that is. (He was no slacker, that Wittgenstein.)

Wittgenstein was a restless sort. After publishing his dense little volume, the young Austrian forsook academia, working at a number of menial jobs, all the while pursuing his thought experiments. When he later returned to teaching, his approach to the philosophy of language had been transformed. He now understood language in a less mathematical, more playful way. His second scholarly book, *Philosophical Investigations*, was compiled by some of his students, based on notes they'd taken during his lectures. Most arresting in that book is Wittgenstein's iconoclastic concept of language games.

Addressing the question of what language is, he compares it to the word game. He poses the question of what various kinds of games—chess, poker, football, word games, solo card games like Solitaire, and military war games—have in common. He's seeking the underlying nature of gameness that defines them all.

It's surprisingly difficult to say what games really are. The younger Wittgenstein engaged in a fastidious search for the kernel of meaning common to all uses of the word *game*. But the older man no longer prized such mathematical certainty. Every word spoken is like a player's move in a game: The way others respond is varied and greatly influenced by the context in which the words are spoken.

We learn the meanings of words, Wittgenstein suggests, in a way akin to how we discern family resemblance. What's at the heart of family resemblance? Is it a single common trait, like a big nose, distinctive ears, or the color of eyes or hair? No, it's none of these things. And yet somehow, mysteriously, it's all of them.

Every word you speak from the pulpit is an invitation, a proffer of meaning. You converse with your people about the most abstract, inscrutable matters: the love of God, the nature of faith, and the meaning of death and what lies beyond it. Yes, it's important for the sake of precision to get your language right, to traffic in recognized theological categories. But far more important to powerful preaching is to avoid slavishly following rules catalogued by theology professors and to know when to judiciously break them.

Bill Watterson's *Calvin and Hobbes* comic strip is beloved by many. From time to time, when the weather is nice—or when it isn't, which is even better—the boy Calvin and his tiger friend, Hobbes, engage in an exuberant game of Calvinball. There's only one rule to Calvinball: No two games of it are alike. In Calvinball, rules can never be used twice (except for the rule that rules cannot be used twice). Any plays made in one game may not be made again in any future games. Game equipment varies. There's usually a ball of some sort, although not always. There may also be wickets, croquet mallets, badminton birdies, buckets, sacks, water balloons, or inscrutably, Lone Ranger masks. One strip introduces the opposite pole. Whenever a player touches it, everything becomes the opposite of what it was before. Players must declare when they touch the opposite pole, but because it's opposite, they declare touching it by not declaring it. The field of play contains "vortex spots," in which players must spin around wildly until they fall down. There are also "invisible sectors." Stumble into one of those, and you must immediately cover your eyes. You can't exit an invisible sector until you've been bonked by the Calvinball.

Did Watterson ever read Wittgenstein? Who's to say? The cartoonist does seem to have a good intuitive handle on how language games operate. How do you win at Calvinball? You win by wearing yourself out in exuberant play, until you trudge back home, arms around each other's shoulders, vowing that today's game is the best you've ever played. Tomorrow, you hope for a free and wide-open day so you can play it all over again. But never, of course, by the same rules.

A well-designed sermon is something like that: Its malleable rules and richly varied implements of play are what illuminates the experience.

THE PREACHER AS DOCENT

An aspect of the museum curator's work is recruiting docents to lead tour groups. *Docent* originates from the Latin *docentem*, "to teach."

Whether a museum employee or a skilled volunteer, a docent's enthusiasm complements any exhibition design. Docents greet patrons and accompany them through the exhibit halls, pointing out highlights and providing background information. In some museums, docents have been replaced by earbuds that present a narration delivered via smartphone. As useful as that technology is, it lacks the personal touch.

The collaborative nature of preaching means you must do more than simply write a moving sermon. You must also present it, live.

The noted actor Alan Alda has had a fruitful second career as a science communicator and consultant. A service he's provided has been to consult with medical students on how they, as physicians, can communicate with their patients more effectively. In an online talk, Alda tells how he deploys an elementary acting exercise: the famous mirror exercise, in which two actors stand facing each other, imagining one of them is the other's reflection in a full-length mirror. The rules say the two must go through the exercise in silence, which makes it a very difficult trick to pull off. (There's a famous TV clip of Harpo Marx as lead actor, mirrored by Lucille Ball. It's hilarious and well worth downloading.)

Alda says success is only possible after two actors have worked together for a while, getting to know each other's habitual movements and facial expressions. Even with that familiarity, they still can't read each other's minds, so the lead actor has to take responsibility for nonverbally informing the mirroring partner what's coming next.[24]

Something similar happens when you're writing sermons. You're the lead actor and you want your listeners to follow your reasoning. As you choose your words, you can't just focus on what you want to say. You also need to ponder how your listeners are likely to receive the message. In choosing words, good communicators constantly switch back and forth between what they want to say (i.e., the word

---

24 Alan Alda, "How to Grow Your Empathy Through Better Visual Perception," *BigThink*, n.d., accessed July 17, 2024, https://bigthink.com/smart-skills/alan-alda-how-to-grow-your-empathy-through-better-visual-perception/.

they would ordinarily choose) and how they imagine their listeners will understand it. If the word's not a good match, just discard it for another. If the reasoning seems too complex, then reach for a likely metaphor. Good preaching—any public speaking, really—is a two-party process.

Screenwriter Robert McKee describes this two-party process as a conspiracy of interest between himself and his movie audience:

> This craft is neither mechanics nor gimmicks. It is the concert of techniques by which we create a conspiracy of interest between ourselves and the audience. Craft is the sum total of all means used to draw the audience into deep involvement, to hold that involvement, and ultimately to reward it with a moving and meaningful experience.[25]

Meaning doesn't reside in the words spoken. It happens dynamically, in the space between speaker and listener. The two parties conspire together to make it happen—although, like the actor leading the mirror exercise, the speaker is the one responsible for making sure it happens. Considering the role the Holy Spirit—the *pneuma*, or breath of God—plays in the process, it's more than interesting that the literal meaning of conspire is to breathe together.

Alda goes on to tell a story about one of the medical students he was working with. The intern was making hospital rounds, shadowing a senior MD. The supervising doctor's task was to inform a woman she had incurable cancer and was soon going to die. As the medical student listened to his instructor delivering this hard news, he was looking intently at the patient's face. It displayed a blank expression, devoid of emotion. He got the strong impression she wasn't understanding what his medical mentor was telling her.

---

25 Robert McKee, *Story: Style, Structure, Substance, and the Principles of Screenwriting* (ReganBooks, 1997), 21–22.

Having delivered his grim prognosis, the senior doctor politely expressed his concern for his patient and told her they'd talk later. As he was turning to leave, the medical student asked him if he could stay a few minutes longer and talk with the patient. His supervisor agreed.

Rather than standing at the foot of the bed, the medical student sat down beside the woman and took her hand in his. He started to repeat the facts the senior physician had told her, but he didn't use the same words. Instead of *metastases*, for example, he talked in simpler terms. But the important thing was that he was making eye contact with her all the while, opening himself up to her. Little by little, she started to cry. She asked questions. Finally, from the light in the patient's eyes, the medical student knew the message had gotten through. She understood what she was up against. At that moment, he, too, started to cry.

> I don't think he was crying because he felt her pain at the awareness that she was going to die. I think he was moved because this connection had taken place, and he realized that the movement he had made during the workshops to be able to make this kind of contact with another person was a profound experience, and he said that he would never forget the experience and how it came from the simple mirroring exercise.[26]

It's essential—not merely in preparing a sermon but also in delivering it—to treat our communication like a mirroring exercise. Ours is the lead role, the guiding role: cueing our listeners with knowledge of what's happening and what's coming next. If something's not getting through, we make adjustments. It's in the sacred, shared space of interpersonal connection that the spark leaps the neural synapse and true communication happens.

---

26 Alda, "How to Grow Your Empathy."

PREACH LIKE A PLAYWRIGHT

I've already spoken of the necessity of abandoning the erudite language conventions of academia that many of us have worked long and hard to perfect. But what do you replace them with?

One answer is to write like a playwright or perhaps a screenwriter. If the purpose of preaching is testimony, and if testimony is a form of conversation, then you must bring to the task a playwright's mastery of dialogue.

There's a familiar story of a notable preacher who used to set an empty chair in front of his desk. As he went about writing his sermons, he envisioned a single individual sitting in that chair: a member of his congregation, perhaps, or even a newcomer. Imagining his sermon as a conversation rather than a lecture, he would ruthlessly pare away any academic jargon that crept into his writing.

Filmmaker Ken Burns shared with a podcast interviewer what it's like to edit the raw footage of a movie scene. It doesn't matter how excellent the first take is, he explained, or how strong the temptation to simply leave it alone. Sometimes it just has to be edited to make it more accessible to the audience. Viewing his raw footage over and over, Burns explained, he strives to hear every story he's telling as though for the first time. "I'm the representative of the audience in every screening. I just go, 'Why are you assuming I know that? Why are you telling me that?'"[27] The trick, Burns is saying, is to constantly shift our field of vision back and forth, between what we're seeking to say and how our people are likely to hear it.

Take special note of Burns's self-description as the representative of the audience. Yes, he produced the raw footage, but as he sits in the darkness of the editing room, he changes his stance. No longer is he speaking to the audience. He's speaking for them.

There's precedent for this in our theology of the Holy Spirit. John 14:16 refers to the Spirit as *paraclete* (*parakletos* in Greek). Paraclete

---

27 Scott Carter, host, *Ye Gods! With Scott Carter,* season 1, episode 22, "Ken Burns, We Hold These Truths," Efficiency Studios, March 29, 2023, https://www.efficiencystudios.org/yegods.

is a transliteration, of course. The original is hard to translate into English, but when translators are so bold as to attempt it, the word comes out meaning "advocate, counselor, or helper." It has origins in the law courts of the ancient world, where defendants would rely on the services of a legal expert—an attorney, essentially—to speak for them.

As preachers, we rely on the inspiration of the Holy Spirit at every stage of the homiletical process. In the editing phase, especially, we model the paraclete's role, advocating to our more verbose selves on behalf of our listeners who are calling out for simple, evocative language. "You know [the paraclete]," John says, "because he abides in you, and he will be in you" (14:17).

Martin Luther followed a similar technique, although he was very particular in imagining his target listeners:

> Cursed be every preacher who aims at lofty topics in the church, looking for his own glory and selfishly desiring to please one individual or another. When I preach here I adapt myself to the circumstances of the common people. I don't look at the doctors and masters, of whom scarcely forty are present, but at the hundred or the thousand young people and children. It is to them that I preach, to them that I devote myself, for they too need to understand. If the others don't want to listen, they can leave.[28]

Great preachers don't talk down to their listeners. They come alongside.

There's a Script in Manuscript

Never forget that in crafting sermons, you're writing for speech. Barbara Brown Taylor—a master of the art—brilliantly explains

---

28 Jaroslav Pelikan and Helmut Lehmann, eds., *Luther's Works,* American ed., vol. 35 (Fortress, 1955), 235.

how her own writing process demands constant revision, an ongoing translation between the printed page and "the air":

> While the words appear first on the page, they are not meant to stay there. They are meant for the ear, not the eye, which turns the page into the stage where the words audition and rehearse. They file in to show me what they can do. I weed them out. They explain themselves to me. I ask for more feeling. They arrange themselves one way. I suggest another. They focus on meaning. I make them give me rhythm. Finally it is my turn to say them out loud, which is when I usually have to let a few more of them go—because what is lovely on the page is often too heavy for the air.
>
> That is only logical if you think about it, since a page is so much more substantial than the air. A page can hold hundreds of words still tethered to one another by commas and semicolons, so that a reader can go back and make sure that none has gotten away. As long as you have a page, you don't need a memory. If you don't get something the first time, then you may go back as many times as you like. The words will be right there waiting for you, as patient as rabbits in a pen.
>
> But none of that works in the air. In order to survive that medium, words have to be fast and light. Pack too many syllables in them and they will sink before they have gone three feet out of your mouth. Link a long string of them together with a semicolon, and watch half of them take a wrong turn because those in the back lost sight of those up front. Or try keeping the words abstract, with no body odor to them at all, and you may also discover that words can be too light for air. Without any smell to them, without any color or heat in them to keep them down to earth, words can float clean out

> of human reach. Even in the air, words need enough ballast to anchor them in memory.[29]

That means using short sentences, avoiding polysyllabic words (such as *polysyllabic*), frequently using second-person pronouns, minimizing marginally necessary words like *that* (which occur in conversation much less frequently than they do in text written for the eyes as opposed to the ears), shunning jargony transition words (*however, furthermore, secondly*), favoring the active over the passive voice, using present rather than past tense in telling stories, and freely using sensory imagery that helps listeners transport themselves down the ladder of abstraction into the scenes you're describing.

Many years ago, the novelist George Orwell famously came up with six basic rules for keeping writing fresh and alive:

> What is above all needed is to let the meaning choose the word, and not the other way about. In prose, the worst thing one can do with words is to surrender to them. When you think of a concrete object, you think wordlessly, and then, if you want to describe the thing you have been visualizing, you probably hunt about till you find the exact words that seem to fit it. When you think of something abstract you are more inclined to use words from the start, and unless you make a conscious effort to prevent it, the existing dialect will come rushing in and do the job for you, at the expense of blurring or even changing your meaning. Probably it is better to put off using words as long as possible and get one's meanings as clear as one can through pictures and sensations. Afterward one can choose—not simply accept—the phrases that will best cover the meaning, and then switch round and decide what impression one's words are likely

---

29 Barbara Brown Taylor, "Way Beyond Belief: The Call to Behold," in *Shouts and Whispers: Twenty-One Writers Speak About Writing and Their Faith*, ed. Jennifer L. Holberg (Eerdmans, 2006), 1–2.

> to make on another person. . . . I think the following rules will cover most cases:
>
> 1. Never use a metaphor, simile, or other figure of speech which you are used to seeing in print.
> 2. Never use a long word where a short one will do.
> 3. If it is possible to cut a word out, always cut it out.
> 4. Never use the passive where you can use the active.
> 5. Never use a foreign phrase, a scientific word, or a jargon word if you can think of an everyday English equivalent.
> 6. Break any of these rules sooner than say anything outright barbarous.[30]

Earlier in the same article, Orwell engages in what he calls a parody to illustrate his point. He does precisely the opposite of what he's been teaching, offering a negative example. Orwell translates the well-known words of Ecclesiastes 9:11 into soulless academic jargon. Here's the biblical original from the Authorized (King James) Version:

> I returned and saw under the sun, that the race is not to the swift, nor the battle to the strong, neither yet bread to the wise, nor yet riches to men of understanding, nor yet favour to men of skill; but time and chance happeneth to them all.[31]

Now here's Orwell's satirical butchering of Koheleth's and the sixteenth-century English translators' art. The problem is not that Orwell's translation is logically inaccurate. It's not. The base-level meaning is still there. But it's like swapping a helium balloon for a cinder block:

> Objective consideration of contemporary phenomena compels the conclusion that success or failure in competitive activities

---

30 George Orwell, "Politics and the English Language," in *The Collected Essays, Journalism and Letters of George Orwell*, ed. Sonia Orwell and Ian Angos, vol. 4 (Harcourt, Brace, Jovanovich, 1968), 139.

31 Orwell, "Politics and the English Language," 133.

> exhibits no tendency to be commensurate with innate capacity, but that a considerable element of the unpredictable must invariably be taken into account.[32]

In the immortal words of actor Strother Martin—playing the character of a chain-gang overseer to actor Paul Newman's convict in the film *Cool Hand Luke*—"What we've got heah is failyuh to communicate."[33]

AN ILLUMINATION TOOLBOX

It may help to identify a few useful writing tools. Because rhetorical language games are so diverse and their boundaries overlap, hard-and-fast categorization is impossible. But here's a list of rhetorical tools, anyway—just a few examples of leading types of illuminations.

Shofar: A blast of the ram's horn at the beginning of the sermon provides an invitation to listen, a call to attention. A story — perhaps apocryphal — has long circulated about the well-known nineteenth-century minister Henry Ward Beecher. On a blisteringly hot summer Sunday, he purportedly began a sermon by mopping his forehead with his handkerchief and saying, "God damn, it's hot! . . . I heard one man say as he came into church today." That's one way of getting a congregation's attention.

Cody Keenan, a speechwriter for President Barack Obama, advises paying close attention to "the handshake at the top of the speech."[34] By this he means mentioning something that establishes common ground with the audience. Whenever the president was speaking at a high school, Keenan always made sure his boss mentioned the name of the school mascot. Once you establish even a trivial connection like that, he says, "then you have the permission structure to take

---

32 Orwell, "Politics and the English Language," 133.

33 *Cool Hand Luke*, directed by Stuart Rosenburg (Warner Brothers, 1967).

34 Cody Keenan, "How to Write a Perfect Speech," November 19, 2019, BBC Ideas, YouTube.com. https://www.youtube.com/watch?v=oV1h7n0HcTE.

the audience on a greater ride."[35] First Lady Michelle Obama began one speech to a London girls' school by saying, "I want to thank all of the students here: the smart, powerful, creative, accomplished young women of Mulberry School for Girls. You all are beautiful!"[36] Both openers implicitly say to the listeners, as Keenan points out, "I know you don't have to pay attention to me today, but if you do, I promise to tell you something worth hearing."[37]

In medias res: An alternative opener is to jump right into a biblical story, either the text for the day or another. Literally, this Latin phrase means "into the middle of things." This approach is especially effective if there's some arresting detail in the story that can grab the congregation's attention.

Bookends: Begin by telling part one of a story and then interrupt it to consider the biblical text and its theological and personal implications. At the end, take up the story again where you left off, so completing the story simultaneously completes the sermon.

Playful: Remember what happened in your elementary school classroom on the first glorious spring day? Who could concentrate on the lesson? Your eyes—along with those of your classmates—were drawn toward the window as though by some magnetic force.

Wise teachers, reading the room, know it's well-nigh impossible to resist that pull, so they give in—but only for a little while. Some humorous stories and jokes directly illuminate the sermon, but others simply provide a brief break in the action. In so doing, they recapture wandering minds and build community.

Curiosities: Facts or trivia items spark curiosity. The facts I've provided in the introduction about where ancient Celtic scribes got their inks and paints are an example. Yes, such details are literally

35 Keenan, "How to Write a Perfect Speech."

36 Michelle Obama, "Remarks by The First Lady at Let Girls Learn Event in London, UK," Obama White House Archives, June 16, 2015, https://obamawhitehouse.archives.gov/the-press-office/2015/06/16/remarks-first-lady-let-girls-learn-event-london-uk.

37 Keenan, "How to Write a Perfect Speech."

beside the point. But they do help incite interest in the point, as long as they're not overdone.

Appeal to authority: These are quotations from famous people saying substantially the same thing as a point you make in the sermon. The shorter the better. As I've said earlier, do be careful to confirm attribution, particularly if your source is social media or the sort of quotations website that provides just the name of a purported source with no documentation.

Via negativa: Provisionally make a point directly opposed to what the biblical text is saying, then debunk it.

Caution tape: This tool is a variation of the *via negativa*. Give an example of what you don't want people to do, by way of contrast.

Time machine rewind: Bring the listener back into the biblical story by means of one or more of the five senses. Here's Buechner describing David's dance before the ark of the covenant in *Peculiar Treasures*:

> David had the ark loaded onto a custom-built cart and made a regular circus parade of it, complete with horns, harps, cymbals, and psalteries, not to mention himself high-stepping out front like the Mayor of Dublin on Saint Patrick's Day. . . .
>
> So far it was none of it anything a good public relations man couldn't have dreamed up for him, but the next thing was something else again. He stripped down to his skivvies, and then with everybody looking on including his wife—a high-class girl named Michal who gave his administration tone as the late King Saul's daughter—he did a dance. Maybe it started out as just another Madison Avenue ploy, but not for long.
>
> With trumpets blaring and drums beating, it was Camelot all over again, and for once that royal young red-head didn't have to talk up the bright future and the high hopes because he was himself the future at its brightest, and there were no hopes higher than the ones his people had in him. . . . How they cut

> loose together, David and Yahweh, whirling around before the ark in such a passion that they caught fire from each other and blazed up in a single flame of such magnificence that not even the dressing-down David got from Michal afterwards could dim the glory of it.
>
> He had feet of clay like the rest of us if not more so—self-serving and deceitful, lustful and vain—but on the basis of that dance alone, you can see why it was David more than anybody else that Israel lost her heart to and why, when Jesus of Nazareth came riding into Jerusalem on his flea-bitten mule a thousand years later, it was as the Son of David that they hailed him.[38]

Time machine fast forward: Move an ancient message forward through time, playfully inserting anachronisms. Here is an example from a sermon of mine:

> Abe sat at the picnic table in his backyard, sipping a cool lemonade. He wiped his brow with the torn T-shirt he was wearing and looked out over his freshly mown lawn.
>
> Sara was of the opinion he shouldn't push the lawnmower himself, at the age of seventy-five. They could certainly afford a lawn service. But Abe enjoyed pushing the mower up and down, tracing the same familiar patterns around the trees and shrubs. He loved the smell of the grass clippings. He loved even more the sense of accomplishment that came with that smell: one more job completed, and completed well.
>
> For Abe, life was good. He'd had a successful career. A long and happy marriage of over fifty years. Money in the bank, always:

---

38 Frederick Buechner, "David," in *Peculiar Treasurers: A Biblical Who's Who* (HarperSanFrancisco, 1979), 22–24.

> more than they needed. Abe and Sara owned their house, free and clear (it had belonged, in fact, to Abe's father before him).
>
> If Abe had any disappointment in life, it was that he and Sara had never managed to have children—but they did see a lot of the nephews and nieces who lived in town (especially that fine young man, Lot, who lived just around the corner).
>
> Sara was seated at the kitchen table, leafing through a pile of real-estate brochures. Each of them depicted one of those adult communities down at the Shore. Maybe this was the year, she told herself, they'd actually do it. Maybe this was the year they'd pound a For Sale sign into the front lawn and simplify their lives. Those glossy photos in the brochures looked awfully tempting, she had to admit: golf course, swimming pool, clubhouse. All the outside maintenance covered by the membership fee. Maybe this was the year they'd make the move.
>
> Sitting at the picnic table in the backyard, nursing that lemonade, Abe hears the Voice. "Go!" says the Voice. That's all it says: "Go!"[39]

Buechner's "Amos," in *Peculiar Treasures*, provides another example:

> When the prophet Amos walked down the main drag, it was like a shoot-out in the Old West. Everybody ran for cover. His special target was the "beautiful people," and shooting from the hip, he never missed his mark. He pictures them sleek and tanned at Palm Beach, Acapulco, St. Tropez. They glisten with Bain de Soleil. The stereo is piped out over the marble terrace. Another tray of Bloody Marys is on the way. A vacationing bishop plunges into the heated pool.

---

39 Carlos E. Wilton, "On the Road," unpublished sermon preached at the Point Pleasant Presbyterian Church, Point Pleasant Beach, NJ, June 6, 1999.

With one eye cocked on them, he has his other cocked on the unbeautiful people—the varicose veins of the old waiter, the pasty face of the starch-fed child, the Indian winos passed out on the railroad siding, the ragged woman fumbling for food stamps at the check-out counter.[40]

You are there: Retell a biblical story through the eyes of a first-person witness, concentrating on sensory detail, as I've done here:

John the Baptist stands knee-deep in muddy Jordan river water, baptizing the hordes of holiness seekers who are dreaming that maybe this man can make a difference in their hardscrabble lives.

Off to one side stands another man, a stranger. He regards the curiously chaotic scene with thoughtful detachment. His face betrays no hint of emotion, but the rapid movements of his eyes—darting from John to each candidate for baptism and back again—indicate his intense interest in what he's seeing.

It's almost as though he's trying to make up his mind—or maybe that he's already made up his mind and is merely waiting for the right moment to join them.

Join them he does, in a little while: slipping and sliding down the muddy bank like all the others, pulling off his sandals, wading into the water until he comes face-to-face with the baptizer. John lowers this mysterious figure backward into the water, and as he emerges, Mark tells us, he sees "the heavens torn apart and the Spirit descending like a dove on him."[41]

---

40 Frederick Buechner, "Amos," in *Peculiar Treasurers: A Biblical Who's Who* (HarperSanFrancisco, 1979), 6.

41 Carlos E. Wilton, "The Heavens Torn Open," unpublished sermon preached at the Point Pleasant Presbyterian Church, Point Pleasant Beach, NJ, January 12, 1997.

The big reveal: Begin an anecdote about a historical figure without revealing who it is until the end. This example is one of those historical anecdotes of uncertain authorship:

> Here's a story about a man who had a hard life. When he was seven years old, his family was evicted from their home. When he was nine, his mother died. At twenty-two, he lost his job as a store clerk. He'd always wanted to go to law school, but his education wasn't good enough. He went into business instead, and at age twenty-three became a partner in a small store. Three years later, his partner died, leaving a huge debt that took him years to repay.
>
> At twenty-eight, he asked the woman he'd been courting for years to marry him. She said no. At thirty-seven, on his first try, he was elected to Congress, but two years later he was voted out. At forty-one, his four-year-old son died. At forty-five, he ran for the Senate and lost. At forty-seven, he failed as the vice presidential candidate. At forty-nine, he ran for the Senate again and lost. At fifty-one, he was elected president of the United States.
>
> His name was Abraham Lincoln. Some people get all the breaks, don't you think?

Compassionate: This tool evokes emotion by telling a very human story whose characters are brought to life in a way that evokes empathy. An example is this story told by Rev. Fred Rogers, Mister Rogers of TV fame, in a May 20, 2001, commencement address at Marquette University. It's a story about a Special Olympics track meet that took place in Seattle:

> For the 100-yard dash there were nine contestants, all of them so-called physically or mentally disabled. All nine of them assembled at the starting line; and, at the sound of the

gun they took off—but one little boy stumbled and fell and hurt his knee and began to cry. The other eight children heard the boy crying. They slowed down, turned around, saw the boy and ran back to him—every one of them ran back to him.

One little girl with Down's Syndrome bent down and kissed the boy and said, "This will make it better." The little boy got up, and he and the rest of the runners linked their arms together and joyfully walked to the finish line. They all finished the race at the same time.

And when they did, everyone in the stadium stood up and clapped and whistled and cheered for a long, long time. People who were there are still telling the story with obvious delight. And you know why, because deep down, we know that what matters in this life is much more than winning for ourselves. What really matters is helping others win, too, even if it means slowing down and changing our course now and then. There's a part of all of us that longs to know that even what's weakest about us can ultimately count for something good.[42]

Phantasmagoric: Introduce, into a rather straightforward story of human experience, some supernatural elements. Craddock has famously done this with a story I'm paraphrasing here:

There was a young woman who learned she had a potentially fatal illness. She had surgery and then some treatments. For a time, she was able to get on with her life: but then, at a routine checkup, she learned the dreaded disease was back.

---

42 Fred Rogers, "Commencement Speech," Marquette University, May 2001, accessed July 17, 2024, https://www.marquette.edu/university-honors/honorary-degrees/rogers-speech.php.

There was more surgery and further treatment. This time it took more out of her. Recovery was slower. But the patient persevered and returned to her life again.

Some years later, during another routine checkup, she learned the disease had once again returned. This time, the prognosis was grim. She spent some time talking with her friends. She prayed. And she decided there would be no more surgery, no more heavy treatments. The young woman went home. Her friends gathered around.

One day, Death came and knocked at the door. Her friends rushed to the door and leaned against it to keep Death out. Death went away.

But Death came back, and this time Death not only knocked but also leaned on the door as though to push it in. The young woman's friends leaned against it all the harder. Death went away.

A short while later, Death came calling again. Death knocked on the door and leaned against the door. The friends made as if to stand against it. But the young woman said, "No, move away." They looked at her as though she were crazy. She couldn't possibly know what she was saying. They refused to obey.

But she told them again, in a louder voice, to move away from the door. When they saw the steely determination in her eyes, they knew she meant what she said, so they moved away. Sensing no resistance, Death pushed open the door and came into the room. The young woman was sitting propped up on pillows, waiting for Death, looking her opponent right in the eye.

When Death saw the strength of her spirit, the intruder looked beaten and ashamed. Death took her but knew that, by the

> power of Jesus Christ and by the witness of the communion of saints gathered there in that room, there was no triumph to be had that day. Death had been beaten again.[43]

Splint: Like a story that includes a subplot, certain stories parallel the master story of the sermon, helping to bring the message home. These function like a first-aid splint supporting a weak leg; they allow the argument to stand upon its feet. Here's one from a sermon of mine about Joseph sacrificing his own pride and prerogatives in order to care for the unexpectedly pregnant Mary and advance his dreamy plan:

> One of the most beloved Christmas stories of all time is "The Gift of the Magi," written by the American short story writer, O. Henry. It used to be a staple of junior-high English-class reading lists.
>
> It's a story about a young couple, Jim and Della, preparing to celebrate Christmas in New York City over a century ago. Each one is determined to find the one perfect gift that will make the other happy. The only problem is this couple has very little money.
>
> Jim's most prized possession is a pocket watch he inherited from his father. But the watch has no chain. Della is determined to buy her husband a fine platinum chain, so that when he takes the watch out of his vest pocket to check the time, he can feel proud.
>
> As for Della, she has her eye set on a pair of beautiful tortoiseshell combs she saw in a department-store window. Her most

43 Adapted from Fred B. Craddock, "Sit at My Right Hand Until . . .," in *Craddock Sermons* (Westminster John Knox, 2011), 210–14.

prized possession is her long hair. She would just love to wear those combs in it.

If you've read the story before, you know what happens. Jim takes his gold watch and sells it so he can have enough money to buy his wife the combs. Della cuts off her long, beautiful hair and sells it to a wigmaker so she can buy her husband the platinum watch chain. On Christmas Day, they exchange two gifts that have been rendered absurdly and utterly useless by the extravagant sacrifice each one has made.

The story ends with Jim and Della reveling in the love they share—love so great it's led them to sacrifice their most cherished possessions for the good of the other. There's a certain sadness to the story as we consider what each one has lost. Yet there's also an abiding sense of joy, as we realize it wasn't about the gifts at all—but, rather, about the giving.

Here's how O. Henry finishes up his quirky, ironic tale:

> The magi, as you know, were wise men—wonderfully wise men—who brought gifts to the Babe in the manger. They invented the art of giving Christmas presents. Being wise, their gifts were no doubt wise ones, possibly bearing the privilege of exchange in case of duplication. And here I have lamely related to you the uneventful chronicle of two foolish children in a flat who most unwisely sacrificed for each other the greatest treasures of their house. But in a last word to the wise of these days let it be said that of all who give gifts these two were the wisest. O all who give and receive gifts, such as they are wisest. Everywhere they are wisest. They are the magi.[44]

---

44 O. Henry, "The Gift of the Magi," in *The Book of Virtues: A Treasury of Great Moral Stories*, ed. William J. Bennett (Simon & Schuster, 1993), 170.

> In that sense, Joseph was one of the magi too. For he gave up his righteousness, his precious reputation as a *tsaddiq*, or holy man, for the sake of his beloved Mary and the child in her womb.[45]

News items: Following Barth's famous encouragement to preach with the Bible in one hand and the newspaper in the other (which made more sense when more people still blackened their fingertips reading print newspapers) the daily news can be a rich source of stories suitable for sermons. These offer the added benefit that listeners may already be familiar with them.

Jesus himself uses this technique (as reported in Luke 13:4) when he mentions to his listeners a recent disaster, the collapse of the Tower of Siloam, an incident we know nothing about today apart from Jesus's mentioning it. The fact that this disaster has been lost to history illustrates the shortcomings of this genre—namely, that most news stories have a short shelf life. They need to be served up fresh, not streaked with freezer burn after years in the database.

Trivial pursuit: Who doesn't love trivia? Presenting factoids to your congregation ignites curiosity, which can then be redirected to less trivial matters. Actually, in the oldest uses of the word, trivia was serious business.

The Latin word *trivium*—the first three of the seven liberal arts—describes the foundational curriculum of medieval universities, consisting of grammar, logic, and rhetoric. Once students had mastered the *trivium*, they moved on to the *quadrivium*, consisting of arithmetic, geometry, music, and astronomy.

See? In talking about ancient universities, I've just presented you with some trivia. But that's not all. That piece of trivia is also an example of the next tool in our toolbox.

Etymology: Presenting facts about the origin of theological and other terms can reveal a great deal about their meaning. Beware of

45 Carlos E. Wilton, "Afraid to Love," unpublished sermon preached at the Light Street Presbyterian Church, Baltimore, MD, December 15, 2024.

spurious word-origin stories, though: There are a lot of them out there. The two-volume *Shorter Oxford English Dictionary* is a reasonably affordable source. For my brother, David Wilton, word origins are a major scholarly pursuit. His book, *Word Myths*, documents and debunks some of the more notorious fake word origins that are in circulation.[46] The "Big List" on his website, www.wordorigins.org, is a go-to location for brief sketches of the actual origins of a great many common words and phrases.

In the following example, the insight that *ghost* meant "soul" to the ancients (and not the wandering spirit of a dead person) is worth sharing. Among other things, it explains why *Holy Ghost*—rather than *Holy Spirit*—turns up in the traditional English translation of the Apostles' Creed:

> The Present-Day English word ghost comes from the Old English *gast*, which carried most of the meanings that the word does today. For instance, *gast* could refer to the apparition of a dead person, which is perhaps the most common sense of the word today. . . .
>
> But *gast* had other senses, many of them akin to the senses of the Latin *spiritus*, meaning breath, soul, spirit. And spirit may be the modern word with the range of meanings closest to that of the Old English *gast*. . . .
>
> Old English even had the idiomatic phrase give up the ghost, meaning to die, that is still used in Present-Day English. The Old English translation of Bede's *Ecclesiastical History of the English People* found in Oxford, Corpus Christi College, MS 279 contains this passage about the death of Aidan of Lindisfarne. . . .

46 David Wilton, *Word Myths: Debunking Linguistic Urban Legends* (Oxford, 2004).

> "And it happened that the holy bishop leaned on a post there outside the church that was set there to support the church and there he gave up his ghost."
>
> Bede's original Latin uses *spiritum uitae exhalaret ultimum* (finally he exhaled the breath of life). . . .
>
> But there are senses of ghost today that did not exist in Old English. For example, there is the verb to ghost, meaning to cut off contact with a person, to suddenly stop returning their calls and texts. This sense is in place by 2010. . . .
>
> If Bede or Ælfric had cell phones, maybe they would have ghosted people too, but then again maybe not. After all, it's hard to avoid people when you live in a monastic community.[47]

You wouldn't share all those scholarly minutiae in a sermon, of course. The key insight is that *ghost* used to mean "soul" rather than some wraith you might encounter on Halloween.

Parabolic: Jesus, of course, is a master storyteller, a purveyor of parables. Those homey stories carry listeners to the intended destination by an indirect, arcing path, much as an artillery shell goes up and over, in the curving path known as a parabola, before coming down precisely where the gunnery officers intended. Craddock describes parabolic preaching in this way:

> Parables are metaphorical and therefore expect an interpretive contribution from the listener. The parable gives freedom of interpretation, and therefore responsibility of interpretation to the hearer. Congregations long accustomed to being told what everything means will likely have lazy ears and will resist this

47 David Wilton, "Ghost/Give Up the Ghost," October 30, 2020, https://www.wordorigins.org/big-list-entries/ghost-give-up-the-ghost.

offer of responsible listening. But in the course of time they will come to accept it as their delightful duty.[48]

An example is a story Craddock tells of how he took his wife, Nettie, to visit his first church, located in eastern Tennessee. Here's a paraphrase:

Fred hadn't been back in years. As he traveled, he remembered a time of controversy in that church. The nearby Oak Ridge National Laboratory was expanding, and new families were moving into the area. Craddock urged the people of this lovely little white-frame church to call on the new people, to invite them to church.

They wouldn't fit in here, was the reply.

A week later, there was a congregational meeting. "I move," harrumphed one of the long-time members, "that in order to be a member of this church, you must own property in the county." The motion passed, over the young pastor's objections.

When Fred and Nettie pulled up to the old church building years later, it looked to be a busy place.[49]

Here's how Craddock concludes the story:

The parking lot was full—motorcycles and trucks and cars packed in there. And out front, a great big sign: Barbecue, all you can eat. It's a restaurant, so we went inside. The pews are against a wall. They have electric lights now, and the organ pushed over into the corner. There are all these aluminum

48 Fred B. Craddock, *The Collected Sermons of Fred B. Craddock* (Westminster John Knox, 2011), Introduction.

49 Fred B. Craddock, *Craddock Stories* (Chalice Press, 2001).

and plastic tables, and people sitting there eating barbecued pork and chicken and ribs—all kinds of people. Parthians and Medes and Edomites and dwellers of Mesopotamia, all kinds of people. I said to Nettie, "It's a good thing this is not still a church, otherwise these people couldn't be in here."[50]

Craddock could have drawn a clear connection between the church leaders' xenophobic fear of newly arrived federal employees sharing supermarket aisles with them and the fact that the congregation would eventually die, its sanctuary repurposed as a barbecue joint. But it's far more powerful to let his listeners draw their own conclusion. Let those who have ears hear.

Visual: Many congregations have screens in the sanctuary, as well as the capacity for reaching worshipers by means of screens at home (either synchronously or asynchronously). This opens up all sorts of possibilities for judiciously using visual images to illuminate sermons. Many listeners major in visual learning and react positively to invitations to interpret great art, whether paintings, sculpture, or photographs.

The most effective use of visual images in sermon illumination is to deploy them sparingly—avoiding the sort of generic clip-art images used in advertising and focusing instead on one or two images you've carefully studied and are prepared to interpret.

For example, look up the backstory of Diego Velázquez's painting *The Kitchen Maid*, also known as *La Mulata* (ca. 1620), now hanging in the National Gallery of Dublin. It was long considered to be a homey depiction of a kitchen maid of African or biracial ancestry pausing at her chores. But a 1933 cleaning revealed a portion of the painting that had become completely obscured under layers of accumulated varnish and grime. When the painting was cleaned, an interior serving window was revealed, connecting the maid's kitchen with a dining room beyond. Seated at the dining-room table

50 Craddock, *Craddock Stories*, 29.

are Jesus and his two traveling companions from the Emmaus Road (Luke 24:13–35).

The cleaning revealed the true subject of the painting, something very different than what art historians had long assumed it to be. Its subject was not a typical Spanish domestic scene at all but rather the supper at Emmaus. As with many religious paintings, the artist depicts the characters dressed in garb of his own time—in this case, seventeenth-century Spain. The woman is doing more than her humble duty as a household servant: She's intently listening as she stands at the kitchen counter, eavesdropping on the religious teaching.

As a *mulata* (*mulatto* in English, or person of mixed ancestry), the maid is an outsider in Spanish culture—a descendant on at least one side of her family of the Muslim moors who used to rule Spain. In the painter's era, most people like her belonged to a permanent servant class. The fact that Velázquez focuses his supper at Emmaus picture on her rather than on the two disciples from the biblical story speaks powerfully to the all-inclusive nature of the Christian gospel.

White space: Sometimes a sermon illumination simply provides a break, a fallow space that allows insight to grow. Just as graphic artists make creative use of white space—avoiding printing images right to the edges of the page—a bit of humor or a brief story can give the congregation a little breathing room.

CHAPTER SEVEN

The Archivist

Preparing for Another Sermon

All good things must come to an end. Even sermons.

When the sermon is ended—not just written but delivered—the preacher deserves some well-earned rest. So, whenever church programming permits, put your feet up. Rest a spell. You've earned a preacher's sabbath.

Not long after that, though—if not Sunday afternoon, then maybe Monday, when the sermon's still fresh in your mind—there's one more thing to do. It only takes a few minutes, but it's essential. You need to archive your sermon. This is the final role in curating sermon illuminations: the archivist.

Museum curators do something similar as they shut down a special exhibition. The artifacts they've carefully assembled go back to one of several places. Some go back into the permanent gallery from which they came. Others are returned to the museum that loaned them. The rest are arrayed on storage shelves or in labeled archival boxes in the museum warehouse, out of the public's sight but available for scholarly research, for future exhibitions, or for loan to other museums.

If you're still in the early years of your preaching ministry, it may be hard to understand the necessity of this final step. After all, aren't sermons ephemeral? Once one's been delivered, isn't it time to pass go without looking back and commence your next trip around the lectionary (or sermon series) game board?

Yes, but the day will soon come when you'll find yourself preaching on the same (or similar) text or topic. You may find the details from an old and nearly forgotten sermon creeping back into your consciousness. You may not even be aware of it, but it happens. If you're not careful, you may find yourself delivering a very similar sermon to the same congregation.

What you're most likely to repeat are your sermon illuminations. And because—if you've chosen good ones—these discrete units of text are easily remembered, some of your congregation may remember them too. In the great scheme of things, that may not be the worst cataclysm, but it can convey the impression that your preaching is less than fresh. Certainly, it's good news we're meant to proclaim. But if you frequently recycle the same sermon elements, your preaching may still be good, but it won't sound much like news.

Maybe you pulled some illuminations for last Sunday's sermon from your database. If so, then simply go back in there and enter last Sunday's date. Maybe there are other illuminations you discovered as part of your research process. If so, then cut those paragraphs from your sermon and paste them into your database. Record not only the date you used them but also topic words or Scripture references to lead you back to them again. On occasions when you suspect you may have shared a story before, you'll find it useful to confirm that you have. Or maybe you'll reuse it in another congregation.

If you simply must reuse something you've previously shared with the same congregation, there's a simple trick that makes it sound fresh: Just admit it. Start out by saying: "I know I've shared this story with you before, but it bears repeating." As long as you don't make a habit of that, no one will fault you for it.

Some sermons may be one-offs— new every Sunday—but preaching is different. Preaching is a long game. Remember the fieldstone wall, constructed slowly and methodically over time (see chapter 5)?

Each foot or two of wall may be a single unit, but then another sermon follows, and another, extending the wall right up until the time when you find yourself offering the table grace at your farewell dinner.

As you move on to a new congregation, you'll appreciate the value of those old sermons: not because you'll be quick to pull them out of the proverbial barrel and preach them as is but because they're snapshots in time of your thinking on that text and topic. Past sermons are a rich vein to excavate for present-day preaching.

Or not. Some old sermons seem hopelessly time bound, addressing the needs of people in one particular place and time. Even so, it does no harm to have them in the database. You can never tell which ones will retain their shimmer far into the future, so it's best to save them all. The Microsoft Access database I use has two separate sections: one for illuminations and another for whole sermons. If you're using a free-form database like Evernote, it's simple enough to add a hashtag indicating that the item is a complete sermon. Just be sure you add topic words as well, in order to point your future self to material within it that could be reused.

The process calls to mind an anonymous poem called "Pangur Bán." The poem is scribbled in the margin of a ninth-century Irish manuscript. Pangur Bán is the name of a cat evidently belonging to a monk who was poring over the manuscript one day. The name roughly translates to "White Pangur." The poet compares this cat's passion for mouse hunting with the monk's single-minded scholarly pursuits. Here's a translation of the ancient Irish text:

I and Pangur Bán my cat,
'Tis a like task we are at:
Hunting mice is his delight,
Hunting words I sit all night.

Better far than praise of men
'Tis to sit with book and pen;
Pangur bears me no ill-will,
He too plies his simple skill.

'Tis a merry task to see
At our tasks how glad are we,
When at home we sit and find
Entertainment to our mind.

Oftentimes a mouse will stray
In the hero Pangur's way;
Oftentimes my keen thought set
Takes a meaning in its net.

'Gainst the wall he sets his eye
Full and fierce and sharp and sly;
'Gainst the wall of knowledge I
All my little wisdom try.

When a mouse darts from its den,
O how glad is Pangur then!
O what gladness do I prove
When I solve the doubts I love!

So in peace our task we ply,
Pangur Bán, my cat, and I;
In our arts we find our bliss,
I have mine and he has his.

Practice every day has made
Pangur perfect in his trade;
I get wisdom day and night
Turning darkness into light.[1]

---

1 Jamie Dedes, "'Pangur Bán': The Gift of a 9th Century Irish Poem Revisited in 'The White Cat and the Monk' & 'The Secret of the Kells,'" *Jamie Dedes' The Poet By Day Webzine*, May 5, 2017, https://jamiededes.com/2017/05/05/pangur-ban-the-gift-of-an-old-irish-poem-retold-and-the-secret-of-the-kells/.

We who dare to take on this audacious mission of proclaiming God's word have two spirits within us. One is the spirit of the scholar: staid, somber, systematic, serious in intent. The other is playful, wild, and free, bubbling over with laughter, eager to pounce on just the right metaphor, story, poetic fragment, or provocative quotation. The first approach flows from systematic thinking; the second, from the font of imagination.

Some are inclined to treat sermon illumination with scholarly disdain, as a lowbrow quest for mere illustrations whose purpose is largely decorative. In truth, if you're going to proclaim good news in ways that earn the respect and attention of your listeners, you need to pursue both tasks with equal passion.

The same can be said for your people in their active listening. The tonsured scribe and the fluffy white cat may seem, at first, an odd pair. But together they display a certain symmetry as they go about their labors. These two are kindred spirits engaged in complementary aspects of the same sacred task. What unites them is a common delight in discovering the shimmer and wondering whether, perhaps, the Holy Spirit could be an active agent in that blessed discovery.

Postscript

I began, many pages ago, by suggesting why you need this book. Now, having reached the end—and assuming you've followed me this far—it's only fair that I share a few words about why I decided to write it.

Why—as I'm approaching the biblical threescore years and ten—have I spent such a large part of my early retirement years writing a book? I could have kicked back and followed the dictates of our pleasure-loving popular culture, wholly devoting my time to the pursuit of vaguely defined "leisure."

The realities of the theological publishing marketplace being what they are, it's not the money (How could it be?). No, it's a different sort of motivation. It's my desire to pass the baton to a new generation of preachers.

In chapter 2, I recalled the seminary preaching elective I took over forty years ago with Ernest T. Campbell. Having retired from regular preaching, Ernie was at a similar place in his career as I now find myself. After he retired from the Riverside Church, no one would have faulted him for withdrawing to a well-earned, leisurely retirement. Instead, he got on a train once a week from New York City to Princeton to teach a new generation of aspiring preachers. Throughout my ministry, I've felt grateful to him for insisting that our class carry around those black pocket notebooks for an entire semester, recording insights for future sermons. It kindled in me a lifelong fascination with converting my ephemeral "That'll preach" thoughts and observations into something a little more durable.

Now, toward the end of my own active preaching career, this book is my attempt to do something similar. The analog era of pocket notebooks is but a memory, but the workings of the human mind are much the same—and digital database technology allows us to be so much more efficient at storing and recalling preachable material. Having noticed a yawning gap in homiletics literature on this subject of sermon illumination, I've swapped the analog baton Ernie passed to me for a digital version and am offering it to you.

I confess to some selfish reasons for writing. Although I'm presently filling the vacant pulpit of the Baltimore church we frequent as a part-time bridge pastor, I know the day will soon come when I'll step out again from behind the pulpit and take up my accustomed place among the congregation. Speaking for sermon listeners everywhere, I'm hoping this book will prove useful to you as you curate shimmering insights arising from your readings and experiences, to enrich your proclamation of the good news. We, your listeners, will thank you for it.

Every trade has its tools. Carpenters have their hammers and screwdrivers, handles worn smooth by decades of use. Chefs carry their meticulously sharpened knives from one kitchen to another. Musicians have their favorite instruments, like Willie Nelson's shockingly battered but beloved acoustic guitar, Trigger. As a child, I remember exploring my retired grandfather's attic and coming upon a black leather case containing the stainless-steel obstetrical instruments he used to deliver thousands of babies over the course of a long medical career. What to do with such cherished tools? It's hard to throw them away, but it's also hard to pass them down to members of a new generation that understandably prefers something shiny and new.

My tools, as a preacher, are a good deal more ephemeral. Books are my tools—and as we've downsized our home, I've donated most of the substantial library I'd accumulated—although preachers of my generation universally complain about how hard it is to find recipients for such weighty volumes among today's seminarians, who've been reared on e-books.

If books have been my tools, then words have been my product. I hope the greater portion of those I've uttered over the years have not gone forth from me empty but have somehow, by the Spirit's gracious intervention, played a part in accomplishing God's purposes.

The mainline Protestant Church seems oh-so-tired these days, beset by powerful generational shifts that have gradually revealed themselves over the course of my entire ministry. The slow membership decline hasn't been easy to watch, and maybe my generation of preachers is partially to blame. I can't help but think, though, that no renewal will be possible unless new generations of preachers commit themselves to discovering the same imaginative fire that illumined the sermons that have touched their own hearts and to preserving some of that sacred fire for their own preaching.

Most of those reading this book, I expect, are children of the Reformation. We are from the part of the Christian tradition that has always sought out and valued the fire of the word. God knows, we need more of that fire in the church today. It's my hope that others will pick up this book and find the same joy in preaching I've discovered over these many years and find fresh ways to communicate that joy to God's people.

Baltimore, Maryland
March 21, 2025